A Day or Two in the Napa Valley

An "Insider's" guide for those planning short visits to California's beautiful Napa Valley

J. Michael Orr

Napa Valley Art Studio
Napa Valley, California

To my wife Joan, who's patience, endurance,
and forgiving spirit over the years has prevailed
during the times of my countless ventures …
and to God for his inspiration, wisdom,
and guidance during the writing of this book.
I give him glory for any success it may achieve

Welcome to the Napa Valley

Vineyard panorama looking West

Contents

Points out factors associated with planning your trip.
Lists the importance of obtaining area tour maps, guides,
and other data in advance. Suggests where to obtain such
information.

Lists activities and events occurring throughout the year,
including the *Mustard Festival, April in Carneros, Chefs
Market,* the famous *Napa Valley Wine Auction,* the *Wine and
Food Festival,* the annual *Harvest / Crush,* plus many other
events and holiday affairs.

Covers the importance of obtaining a *Winery Tour Map*
in advance and how to secure one. Lists types of lodging
available plus locations throughout the region. Suggests
ways to research and obtain lodging. Points out lodging
options for the budget minded and where they are located.
Lists RV parks.

Examines steps to take when arriving by automobile or
commercial airlines. Points out roads to take and how to
avoid Bay Area *grid lock* traffic. Suggests alternative arrival
points during various days of the week. Lists best days of
the week to visit. Points out time saving tips if arriving on
weekends.

Points out the difference in temperatures in the Napa Valley and Bay Area throughout the year. Lists expected weather in the Napa Valley. Suggests wearing apparel for the Bay Area and Napa Valley.

Defines *Appellations* or *"growing regions"* in the Napa Valley. Directs the reader to sources of additional information. Defines the term *Sparkling Wine*. Lists major *Sparkling Wine* producers. Points out the four main items printed on wine labels, with an in depth definition of each. Stresses importance of labels as *"guides only."* Explains the bottling process at wineries.

How is it done? Is there a special technique? Explains nuances associated with tasting wine. Covers the *Basics of Wine Tasting*, including appearance, color, swirling, sniffing, and tasting. Suggests tasting alternatives such as *Home Wine Tastings* and local wine shop tastings. Lists the importance of *Wine Ratings*, how they're done, plus sources of information on the subject.

Defines small, medium, and large wineries. Points out factors that might determine what routes to take and what days of the week to visit. Lists routes to follow for traffic avoidance. Suggests different plans for touring depending upon days visited.

Appointments required or not? Explains the difference between *Public* and *Private* wineries. Covers visitation guidelines. Lists tasting fees charged and why they vary. *Are complimentary tastings offered?* If so, how to obtain. Explains *Private Tastings.* Points out importance of calling ahead prior to visits. Explains importance of using a current *Winery Tour Map.* Explains how *Guided Tours* work at *Public* and *Private* wineries. Points out tour options including limos, tour buses, private tours, plus advantages and disadvantages of each. Lists tour fees. Explains *Self Guided Tours* and how they work. Lists information on winery *Cave Tours.* Suggests alternatives for group or corporate events. Explains process for purchasing and shipping wine. Defines wine clubs, how they work and advantages to membership. Explains how wine can be purchased on a *Futures* basis.

Lists some restaurants and gourmet delis throughout the region. Points out importance of making advance reservations. Explains where and how to obtain picnic lunches. Suggests methods for ordering picnic lunches in advance. Lists popular winery offering gourmet deli, picnic facility, and more. Covers other winery picnic facilities open to the public and how to use them.

Suggests other things to do in the area, including mud baths, balloon rides, wine train, bike rides, golf, Bay Link Ferry to San Francisco, auto races, and the Napa Opera House. Points out activities for children and teens to do including bike rides, Marine World Park, Jelly Belly Candy Company, and more.

Lists sample day tours, winery phone numbers, addresses, web sites, directions, tasting and tour fees, appointments needed or not. Points out time saving steps to make your day more enjoyable. Suggests lunch alternatives. Gives a brief description of wineries plus the unique things each has to offer including art exhibits, tram rides, gardens, country vistas, and more. Includes a cooking demonstration class at the " CIA "- Culinary Institute of America. Suggests how to *build* your own Wine Tour, applying proven time saving methods. Lists reasons why wineries are not on tour maps, and how to find them. Points out alternate tours one can arrange on their own.

Lists *Off the Beaten Path* wineries, *Carneros Region* wineries, plus an extensive list of approximately 100 wineries and other facilities to visit.

Lists sources of information including phone numbers and web sites.

Foreword

Have you ever thought about visiting California's beautiful Napa Valley? Of course you have. That's why you purchased this book. Maybe you've talked with a friend or relative who visited the area. What they say is true. It's a fascinating place with quaint towns, vineyard panoramas, outstanding weather, wonderful restaurants, country inns, and of course, world class wineries. Chances are you've already done some research. Maybe you've read another book, or gone on line and looked up the area. Or what about those television travel and cooking shows that highlight the region? Plenty there to whet your appetite for fun and adventure. *But I don't know what wineries to visit, or how its done, or where to stay, or what to do. Can I bring my children? Is there anything for them to do? What's the best time to come? What does it cost? Is there anything else to do besides visiting wineries?* No problem, the information herein will answer these questions and more.

As you may already know, the *Napa Valley* is one of the premier destination points in the world. As a result, it can become crowded during certain times of the year. A recent study by the *Napa Valley Vintners Association* estimated approximately 3 million people visit the region annually. That's a hefty load of people visiting a geographical area 25 miles long and only 1 to 3 miles across in most places. Those unfamiliar with the area's road systems, short cuts, and geography can easily find themselves bogged down in traffic or long lines, a scenario not conducive to an enjoyable visit. Sound bleak? Not to worry. The information in this book will help avoid the problems most experience.

First, let's set the stage by defining the typical visitor to the Napa Valley. Most spend only one or two days in the area. They've done some planning, but may still be confused about where to go and what to do. Maybe they're attending a Bay Area conference, or are in on other business. Having a free day, they decide to drive to the Wine Country and check it out. Or they're on vacation and decide to spend a day or two touring the area. Many ultimately end up at Visitors'

Centers or Tourist Bureaus where they'll receive accurate and helpful guidance. However, others are seeking the same advice ... especially on weekends. Better to do your homework in advance than to stand in long lines waiting to receive information you can obtain early on. Or maybe your one of those truly organized persons, having already planned your trip. You've studied the travel books, have your tour maps, set up your schedules, obtained lodging, and have all your ducks in a row. There may be a few tricks here for you as well.

Unfortunately, without a specific plan, many first time visitors end up at the same places others are visiting. There's so much more to see and do, including quaint country wineries offering marvelous atmosphere's and outstanding wines. These rare gems are out there just waiting to be explored. Better yet, they welcome new visitors and are easy to find. Many will be highlighted in the forthcoming pages.

Vineyard at Goosecross

© Goosecross Winery

Introduction

Having conducted hundreds of private wine tours over the years, author J. Michael Orr is well aware of the pressures one faces when considering a brief visit to California's *Napa Valley Wine Country*. With so little time to spend, one can easily become frustrated when deciding where to go and what to do. Finally, a book devoted to the needs of the short term visitor, providing simple time saving steps to take prior to and during brief visits. So get out your magic marker, find a quiet place, and prepare yourself for a wonderful *Napa Valley Experience!*

Signature Chapter - Part 12

"Sample Day Tours" ... anyone can take

As already noted, planning such a visit can present certain obstacles. Deciding where to go and what to do on brief visits can be time consuming. To address this issue, the author has organized ten *"Sample Day Tour"* itineraries highlighted in *Part 12*. Simply choose a tour, make a phone call or two prior to arrival, then merely show up and follow the itinerary selected. The tours are organized to help you get the most from your visit.

Prologue

Many books have been written about the Napa Valley, each addressing an array of subjects including the evolution of the area and its wineries, grape varieties, vineyard management, the winemaking process, agriculture, prominent persons, soil and weather conditions, and more. These subjects will not be covered here in any great detail. Rather, the information herein will emphasize specific *Time Saving Steps* to take prior to and during brief visits, steps that will help avoid the problems many experience on such visits.

A SHORT HISTORY OF THE NAPA VALLEY

The name "Napa" is a word derived from the language of the Wappo Tribe of Native Americans who once shared the lush green valley with deer, grizzly bears, elk, and mountain lions. The first recorded exploration of the area was led by Padre Jose Altamira in 1823. At that time, the population was estimated to be approximately three to six thousand natives.

In the 1830's, the Napa Valley became one of the first area's in California to be settled by American farmers. In 1848, the actual city of Napa was laid out by Nathan Coombs on property he acquired from Nicholas Higueras Rancho Entre-Napa, an 1836 Land Grant.

When California was granted statehood in 1850, the Napa Valley was in the territory known as the "District of Sonoma." During that time, counties began to be organized. Napa became one of the original 27 counties of California with the city of Napa as the County Seat. It was the gold rush of the early 1850's that really caused the Napa Valley to grow. Severe winters in the gold fields caused miners to seek warmer refuge. The Napa Valley was a natural choice. There was ample work on local cattle ranches and in the lumber industry.

By 1870, the white man had inhabited the valley and the Native Americans who once roamed freely were wiped out by small pox and other diseases.

The Napa Valley is now known mostly for its premium wines. In the beginning, white settlers planted vineyards with cuttings supplied by Catholic priests from Sonoma and San Rafael. In 1861, Riesling cuttings were introduced to the valley. From these small beginnings, the Napa Valley has become one of the premier wine making regions of the world.

In 1880, while on his honeymoon, Robert Louis Stevenson wrote the following description of his experience while riding a train through the Napa Valley:

"A great variety of oaks stood severally in a becoming grove, among the field and vineyards. The towns were compact, in about equal proportions of bright new wooden houses among great and growing forest trees. The chapel bell on the engine sounded most festively that sunny Sunday, with the townsfolk trooping in their Sunday's best to see the strangers. The sun was sparkling on the clean houses, with great domes of foliage humming overhead in the breeze."
—R. L. Stevenson, The Silverado Squatters, Boston 1895
                         —Source - Napa Chamber of Commerce

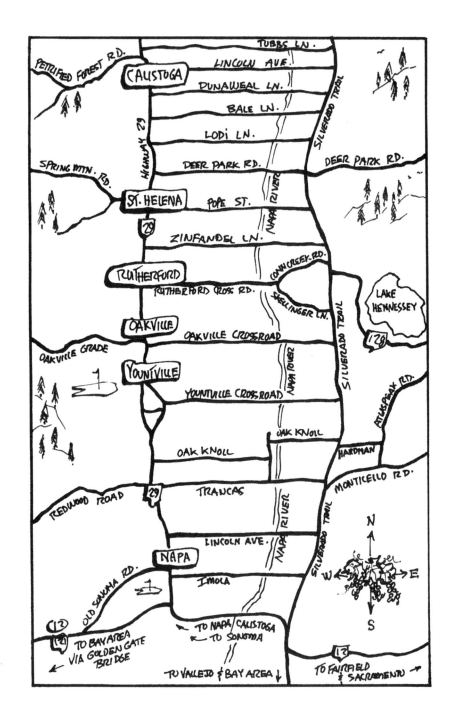

Napa Valley, California

Part 1

Obtaining Information

To begin, it's important to obtain some form of *Tour Map* or *Guide* prior to your visit. Unfortunately, many visitors arrive having done little planning, joining the lines of people at *Tourist Centers* seeking advice. Still others drive directly to a winery, only to find the facility requires a prior appointment, or is closed to the general public for a *Special Event*. A little planning in advance will save a great deal of time, frustration … and money! So, what's the first step in planning a day or two in the Napa Valley? *Get a good tour map and do some homework.*

There are many maps and guides available. A good one will list wineries, their locations, hours of operation, phone numbers, tour and tasting data, and whether appointments are required. Some maps and guides are free. Others are available for a nominal fee. *But remember this when it comes to maps and guides.* There are over 300 wineries in the area. Some are not open to the public. They don't want to be on maps and basically don't want people showing up at their doorsteps. Others may be open to the public on an exclusive basis, but don't want to be on any maps. However, don't be discouraged. Most wineries in the area are open on a walk-in basis or by appointment. If you desire to visit a winery not listed on a current map, go on line and key in their name. Most wineries have web sites. You could also find their phone number by calling area code 707 information for the towns of Napa, Yountville, Oakville, Rutherford, St. Helena, or Calistoga. Lastly, contact any of the local Chambers of Commerce or Visitors Bureaus listed in the directory at the end of this book.

Maps - Two Important Points - **Make sure the map is current and make sure you can read it!**

Make sure it's current.

Many newsprint publications are printed with maps in them, but not necessarily updated. It's not unusual for a winery to change hours of operation or tasting / tour data periodically. They may even change their name. So, obtain a *"current"* map or guide.

Make sure you can read it.

Think about this. Your driving through the beautiful Napa Valley countryside on your way to your first stop. Suddenly, you turn to your companion and ask, *Is this the right road to Clos Du Val Winery?* Wouldn't it be great if they had an eye friendly map at hand, one that was easily read while driving down the road. *Yep, we're on the right road, it's just up ahead on the right!*

Often, newsprint guides are printed in such small type they require a magnifying glass and a searchlight to decipher them. Try reading one of these small print guides while driving down the road. Good luck! What's more, the publishers of these guides feel obligated to include a myriad of other unrelated information, including tons of advertisements and the latest recipe on how to cook zucchini bread. In addition, what about us old folks who need binoculars and radar to find anything in front of us. Give me a map that tells me what I need to know, has big type, is relatively current, and can be easily read while motoring down the road. You guessed it. Here's a chance to pitch my own guide. Check it out at *www.napavalleytourmap.com*. To my knowledge, it's the only locally endorsed winery tour map in the area. You can order it directly from my web site.

Other guides and maps can be obtained by contacting local Chambers of Commerce or Visitors' Centers. Phone numbers and web site addresses are located in the directory at the end of the book. Additional information may be obtained on the Napa web site at *www.napavalley.com*. But no matter where you obtain your *Winery Tour Map*, get it early and use it to plan your visit.

Part 2

Times of the Year to Visit

EVENTS CALENDAR

Wine is always in, so anytime is a good time to visit the Wine Country. There's always something going on, including special events, festivals, and the popular *Harvest / Crush* in the fall. Do some research on line prior to your visit. You can also contact a local Chamber or Visitor Center for information. Let's check out the different times of the year to see what's offered. With so many things happening, you might consider visiting more often.

January

One of the slowest months in the Wine Country. The vines are bare, the crush is long over and people are just getting over Christmas and New Years. Now it's time for tax planning and all that boring stuff. Sounds like a great time for some wine tasting! You can visit on a weekend or weekday with plenty of elbow room. Nothing like tasting the warmth of a world class Cabernet on a brisk January day!

February

Basically the same as January. Vines getting ready to bud. Activity preparing for the new season. Brilliant mustard plants growing amongst the vineyards, soon to form a stunning yellow carpet across the valley floor.

MUSTARD FESTIVAL
An annual event beginning with a three month celebration of the *Mustard Season*. Contact the Yountville Chamber for events occurring this time of the year.

March

Weather warming up. Spring in the air! Vines usually budding full this month. Wild flowers starting to bloom. A wonderful time to visit the Napa Valley. *Mustard Festival* still in full swing.

April / May

One of the most beautiful times of the year. Generally great Spring weather. Wild flowers abound. Vines maturing, income tax time over! School not yet out. Summer vacations yet to begin. Time for some wine tasting in beautiful surroundings. But remember, others are aware of this special time as well. If planning to visit during *April* or *May*, plan well in advance. If staying in the Napa Valley over night, obtain your lodging early. We'll cover lodging alternatives shortly. In addition, try to visit during the week … Monday through Thursday. Much less crowded. If weekends are your only alternative, that's OK. Just plan ahead using the steps covered in this book.

APRIL IN CARNEROS

An open house affair at wineries in the famous *Carneros Region* of the Napa Valley. Contact the Napa Chamber for further information.

MEMORIAL WEEKEND SPRINT CAR RACES

Held in Calistoga. A lot of fun for avid race fans.

CHEFS MARKET

Friday evenings in downtown Napa. The market begins in May, continuing through Labor Day. Plenty to experience including food, wine, entertainment, and more.

FARMERS MARKET AT COPIA

The Farmers Market is an ongoing market open to the public on Tuesday's and Saturday's from May through October. Tuesday's - 7:30 a.m. to 12:00 noon. Saturday's - 8:30 a.m. to 12:00 noon. Check it out for outstanding produce plus much more. 500 First Street, Napa.

June - September

Typical summer months. Great weather, and plenty of visitors. If possible, try to come during the week. However, if weekends are your only option, start your day early *AT THE TOP OF THE VALLEY,* and begin by working your way *DOWN THE VALLEY.* We'll cover this plan later and show you how it's done.

NAPA VALLEY WINE AUCTION

The gala event of the year takes place in June. The auction draws interest from around the world. Details can be obtained on line at *www.napavalley.com* or by contacting any of the local Chambers of Commerce.

WINE AND FOOD FESTIVAL

Annual event held in June sponsored by Hospice of Napa. The festival includes wine tasting, food, live music, and a silent auction. Tickets can be obtained at *www.hospiceofnapa.org.*

CLASSIC CARS AUTO SHOW

Annual June event held in the town of Yountville. Food, live music, and much fun.

WINE COUNTRY FILM FESTIVAL

A July event to consider.

JULY 4th FIREWORKS THROUGHOUT THE COUNTY

NAPA COUNTY FAIR

Held in the town of Calistoga during July.

NAPA TOWN & COUNTRY FAIR

August event held in the town of Napa.

CHAMBER MUSIC

Conducted at various wineries in August. Contact the Napa Chamber or the Napa Valley Conference & Visitors Center for information.

September - October

ANNUAL HARVEST AND CRUSH

One of the most exciting times of the year. The weather is usually beautiful, vacations are pretty much over, the kids are back in school (or are they?), and summer is winding down. However, wonderful things are still happening in the Napa Valley. It's *Crush Time!* The grapes are ready to be picked and it's a magical time in the region. The harvest can occur as early as August and go right into November. You obviously must plan your visit according to your schedule, so hopefully you're in the area when the harvest occurs. Once it begins, it can last for weeks. During this time, the fruit is being transported back and forth across the valley to be crushed at various wineries. The air is filled with a wonderful aroma as the valley bristles in anticipation of the coming vintage. A great *Napa Valley Experience* if you can catch it at the right time.

CALISTOGA BEER, SAUSAGE FEST, AND CHILI COOK OFF

Check out this fun event held during September in the town of Calistoga.

YOUNTVILLE DAYS PARADE AND FESTIVAL

Held during October in Yountville.

OLD MILL DAYS FESTIVAL

An October event in St. Helena highlighting the *Old Bale Grist Mill* north of the city.

November

The grapes have been harvested and the crush is about over. But as usual, every month has something wonderful to offer. In this case, beautiful fall colors in the vineyards! In addition, some marvelous weather is also possible. The grape leafs have turned from their rich summer greens to the vivid reds, golds, and yellows of fall. The vineyards become an endless carpet of colors throughout November into December. Weather permitting, one of the best times of the year to visit. But remember, Thanksgiving week can be busy, so plan ahead.

HOLIDAY IN CARNEROS
An open house event featuring wineries in the *Carneros Region*. Check with the Napa Chamber for details.

FESTIVAL OF LIGHTS
Holiday street faire and tree lighting in the town of Yountville. Check with the Yountville Chamber of Commerce for schedules.

HOLIDAY PARADE
Downtown Napa. Again, check with the Napa Chamber for schedules.

December

Generally a slow winter month. But wine warms the body and heart on a brisk winters day! Christmas week can be a bit busy, so call in advance for events occurring during this time of the year.

CAROLS IN THE CAVES
Holiday caroling at selected wineries. Check out *www.napavalley.com* or contact the local Chambers or Visitors Centers for information.

OPEN HOUSE AND TREE LIGHTING
Downtown Napa. Check for schedules and events.

CANDLELIGHT TOURS OF HISTORIC HOMES
Again, check with the Napa Chamber of Commerce for times and schedules.

ONGOING EVENTS
The following is a brief list of *Ongoing Events* throughout the year, current at the time of publication. Call the phone numbers or check the web sites to verify current status. In addition, another reliable source is the *Napa Valley Conference & Visitors Bureau -707-226-7459.*

Winery of the week at COPIA
Complimentary tasting 12:00 to 4:00 p.m.
Meet the winemakers on Saturdays - 12:00 to 2:00 p.m.
1-800-512-6742 - *www.copia.org*

COPIA's Film Festival
> Friday night flicks - $6.00 general admission at time
> of publication
> 1-888-512-6742 - *www.copia.org*

Cabernet Flight Tasting at a Dozen Vintners
> Taste award winning Cabernets - $5.00 per person at time
> of publication
> 707-967-0666
> *www.adozenvintners.com*

Zinfandel Flight Tasting at a Dozen Vintners
> Taste award winning Zinfandels
> 707-967-0666
> *www.adozenvintners.com*

ZD Wine and Cheese Seminar
> Includes a visit to the Wine Library
> Every Saturday and Sunday morning at 11:00 a.m.
> Cost per person - $20.00
> 1-800-487-7757

Wine Basics Class at Goosecross Cellars
> Every Saturday - 11:00 a.m. to 12:30 p.m.
> Cost - Complimentary
> 1-800-276-9210

Barrel Tasting at Monticello Vineyards
> Third Saturday of the month 11:00 a.m.
> Appointment required - $25.00 per person
> 1-707-253-2802

Live Music at Stomp Restaurant
> Friday and Saturday nights - 9:00 p.m. to 12:00 midnight
> Location - Mt. View Hotel and Spa, 1457 Lincoln Ave., Calistoga
> 707-942-8272 - *www.stomprestaurant.com*

Part 3

Important Steps to take in Advance

Napa Valley Tour Map or Guide

Just another reminder to obtain a winery map or guide in advance. The guide should list roads, directions to wineries, phone numbers and other pertinent information. The directory in the back of the book lists where you can obtain one.

Chambers of Commerce and Visitors Centers

For current information, call these organizations directly or go to their web sites listed in the directory.

Napa Valley Web Site

You can check out just about everything necessary to help plan your trip at *www.napavalley.com*

LODGING

If planning to stay overnight in the Napa Valley, *PLACE THIS ITEM AT THE TOP OF YOUR PRIORITY LIST.* Because of the region's popularity, lodging is at a premium. This is especially true on weekends and during the summer. *SO OBTAIN LODGING WELL IN ADVANCE.* You won't be sorry.

Knowledgeable visitors plan early in the year for Spring, Summer, and even Fall trips. Proprietors of B&B's, hotels, inns, and resorts are well aware of the importance of early booking. Lodging can also be expensive, especially during the popular months and most assuredly on weekends. In this regard, check out the various establishments on line, and look for any *Internet Lodging Specials* that may be offered. Lastly, if you plan to come on a weekend, call well ahead. Many hotels require a two night minimum stay on weekends. So get your lodging booked ASAP! You won't regret it.

Types of Lodging and Locations

Generally, the types of lodging include hotels, motels, inns, B&B's, resorts, cabins, and private homes. Prices vary depending upon amenities offered. Most establishments are located up and down the valley in the towns of Napa, Yountville, Oakville, Rutherford, St. Helena, and Calistoga. A day or two touring the area can easily begin from any of these locations. Research lodging at *www.napavalley.com*. Once there, click on lodging, the city or town, then navigate around to check out the alternatives.

Let's briefly describe the communities in the area to see what they offer. For more in depth information, go to the Napa web site. All of these communities are located along *Highway 29*, the main artery going through the valley.

Napa
The first city one enters when arriving from the south. It has it's main streets, shops, theaters, restaurants, and other normal businesses. Although not situated directly among the vineyards, it's only about 10 to 15 minutes in any direction from the edges of vineyard panoramas and wineries.

Yountville
About 15 minutes up the road from Napa, this small resort community borders on vineyards and beautiful country vistas. The town offers marvelous lodging and spa accommodations, but at a premium price. So be ready. *You're in the Napa Valley!* If staying in Yountville, you're also within easy walking distance to shops, galleries, restaurants, and parks. Check out the lodging options at *www.yountville.com*.

Oakville
The small community of Oakville is located just north of Yountville. The famous *Oakville Grocery* is located here, a great stopover for a snack

or gourmet picnic lunch. There are also a few B&B's and Country Inns in the area. Research these on line.

Rutherford

Located in the heart of the region, Rutherford has some B&B's and Country Inns, plus beautiful vineyard panoramas.

St. Helena

The second largest town in the valley. A beautiful community with stately old mansions, tree lined streets, shopping, galleries, restaurants, outstanding hotels, B&B's, and much more. Check out available accommodations on line or contact the St. Helena Chamber of Commerce.

Calistoga

About 15 minutes above St. Helena is the small town of Calistoga, the northern most community in the region. Famous for it's *Mineral Hot Springs* and *Mud Baths*, it has several hotels offering hot mineral pools, mud baths, and massages. Very popular, so reserve early. In addition, there are wonderful restaurants in the area, all within easy walking distance. Go on line and do your research.

Lodging for the Budget Minded

Less expensive lodging is available in the cities of *Vallejo* and *Fairfield*, only 30 minutes away. Do your research for Vallejo by calling the *Vallejo Chamber at 707-644-5551* or visit *www.vallejochamber.com*. Research for *Fairfield* can be done by calling the *Fairfield Chamber at 707-425-4625*. As phone numbers and web sites can change, verify this information for accuracy.

RV Parks

There are only a few RV parks in the Napa Valley, plus some at *Lake Berryessa*, about 45 minutes away. *RV Parks* in the region are listed here. For more details, go to *www.napavalley.com* and type in the letters RV. *Bothe Napa Valley State Park* 3801 St. Helena Hwy., North St. Helena. 707-942-4575
Napa County Fairgrounds 1435 Oak Street, Calistoga. 707-942-5111
Skyline Wilderness Park 2201 Imola Avenue, Napa. 707-252-0481
Napa Valley Exposition 575 Third Street, Napa. 707-253-4900

Part 4

Method of Arrival - Best Days to Visit

Method of Arrival - Automobile

Make sure to use a *California State Map*. There are three major routes leading into the Napa Valley. One from the south, one from the east, and one from the west. Most visitors arrive from the southern Bay Area. Others arrive from the west via *Highway 101*, then through the Sonoma Valley. Still others arrive from the east via *Highway 80* from the Sacramento, Vacaville, and Fairfield areas. The region is easy to find. Just refer to your California map and follow the road signs.

We'll concentrate on the southern approach first, the one most visitors use. You'll either drive in from the East Bay / Oakland Bay Area, or the San Francisco side of the bay. It's about an hour's drive, but allow an hour and one half.

From Oakland, get on *Highway 80* passing Berkeley, then eventually go over the Benicia Carquenez Bridge passing the town of Vallejo. Shortly past Vallejo, you'll be directed to the right, then back up over the freeway on up to the Napa Valley.

From San Francisco, you'll have two choices. Take the Oakland Bay Bridge, following the directions listed above, or take the Golden Gate Bridge up *Highway 101* where you'll eventually be directed to a right turn toward Sonoma and Napa. Follow the signs through the Sonoma area into the southern Napa Valley.

Visitors arriving from the Sacramento area also have an easy route to follow. Drive down *Highway 80* past the town of Fairfield. Eventually, you'll see the sign to the Napa / Sonoma area's to the right. Follow the signs into the Napa Valley, about 20 minutes from the turn off.

Method of Arrival - Commercial Airlines

Unless your obligated to fly into the Bay Area, consider flying into the *Sacramento Airport* instead. It's a much easier transition and about the same distance to the Napa Valley as from the Bay Area.

If arriving on a weekday, book your flight to arrive in Sacramento between 8:00 a.m. and 11:00 a.m. if possible. This way, you'll have a better chance of missing major commuter traffic after leaving the airport. Drive directly to *Highway 80*, then down to the Napa / Sonoma turnoff to the right. Once you take the turnoff, it's about a 20 minute drive into the Napa Valley.

If arriving at the San Jose, San Francisco, or Oakland airports, follow the directions already noted. However, equally important is the day and time of your arrival. If arriving on a weekday, book your flight to arrive between 8:00 a.m. and 11:00 a.m. This way, if planning on driving to the Napa Valley immediately thereafter, you'll miss the major morning and afternoon Bay Area commuter traffic. However, if your plans include arriving at a Bay Area Airport after 1:00 p.m. on a weekday, then driving to the Napa Valley shortly after your arrival the same day, my prayers are with you! Ever heard of *Road Rage?* That's what you'll have! Afternoon weekday traffic in the Bay Area is a nightmare … no matter what direction you're traveling. In this case I would suggest spending the rest of the day in the Bay Area. Have dinner, go to a movie, visit Fisherman's Wharf, whatever … just don't inject yourself into the late afternoon weekday Bay Area traffic! You'll regret it. Instead, think about driving to the Napa Valley much later in the day or early evening. *You'll thank me!*

Napa does have a small airport, but doesn't accommodate large commercial traffic. If arriving by private plane, check out the flight details for the *Napa Airport* at *Bridgeford Flying Services, 1-888-920-2359 - www.bfsnapa.com*

Best Days to Visit

Plan your visit for a Monday through Thursday if possible. In addition, consider skipping major holidays. However, if visiting on a weekend or major holiday is your only option, follow the steps and shortcuts in this book for a less complicated visit.

If a weekend is your only alternative and your arriving on Friday, try to arrive in the Napa Valley before 2:00 p.m. The region is one of

the Bay Area's most desirable places to live. Commuters are on their
way home from Bay Area work places in the late afternoon. If you
don't arrive in the area before 2:00 p.m., you'll be in the midst of
major traffic. *Not fun!*

Fridays can be equally busy going out of the valley. Locals are
hitting the roads for the weekend. So, consider these factors when
planning your day and time of arrival. The wineries are open daily,
with the exception of a few closed on major holidays, so it really
doesn't matter what day you visit. However, if your fortunate enough
to have a choice, I've always felt Tuesday's and Wednesday's were best.
They always seem to be a bit quieter and less crowded.

Vineyard panorama looking East

Part 5

Local Area Weather...What to Wear

Weather in the Napa Valley & Bay Area

Most visitors initially arrive in the Bay Area, then drive to the Napa Valley. The region is just a short distance from San Francisco. However, it's not uncommon for the weather in the Bay Area to differ vastly from that in the Napa Valley. I believe it was Mark Twain who said one of the coldest days he ever experienced was a July day in San Francisco, or something like that. For example, during the summer, it's not unusual for the temperature in San Francisco to be 20 degrees lower than in the Napa Valley. If arriving in the Bay Area, check out the weather and dress accordingly.

Generally, the weather in the Napa Valley is comfortable throughout the year. It does rain off and on from November through March. However, it's usually quite tolerable. April / May weather is normally beautiful. June through September averages about 80+ degree's, but can get much hotter traveling north up the valley. September and October can be equally beautiful in both the Bay Area and Napa Valley. In summary, the region has some of the best weather in the country, with very little humidity during the summer. Usually beautiful days and pleasant evenings.

What to wear

Temperatures vary from the 50's in winter to the 90's in summer, with average summer temperatures around the 70's to mid 80's. Dress is casual; shorts, tee shirts or polos during warmer months. Very few businesses require any form of dress code. Things are pretty laid back in the area, but bring along one conservative outfit just in case. In addition, a sweater might be a good idea, especially if a *Cave Tour* at a winery is in order. So dress for cool foggy weather in San Francisco during summer months, but bring along those shorts, tee shirts, and polos for a big surprise when you arrive in the Napa Valley.

Part 6

Appellations - Sparkling Wine What's in a Label?

Napa Valley Appellations

At the time of publication, 15 grape growing regions were established in the greater Napa Valley. Commonly referred to as *Appellations*, each has it's own unique climate and soil conditions for growing specific varieties of grapes. The *Carneros Appellation* in the south is the coolest. Closer to the Bay Area, cool air funnels into this region providing the perfect atmosphere for Chardonnay and Pinot Noir grapes. In the north, the famous *Stags Leap Appellation* is warmer, it's climate and soil conditions more conducive to producing outstanding Cabernet Sauvignon, Merlot, and Zinfandel grapes. If interested in finding out more about the *Appellations* in the area, do some research on the Napa web site, or contact a local Napa Valley Chamber or Visitors' Bureau.

Sparkling Wine (Champagne)

Several renowned *Sparkling Wine* producers are located in the region, including *Domaine Carneros, Domaine Chandon, Mumm Napa Valley, Schramsberg, Frank Family, and Cliff Lede*. Normally, these would be referred to as *Champagne* producers. However, the French were the first to produce true *Champagne*, their method historically outdating all others. In deference to the French, it is common practice to refer to local American premium Champagne as *Sparkling Wine*. In this regard, you won't see the word *Champagne* on any premium wine produced in the Napa Valley.

When planning a visit, consider a *Guided Tour* at one of the *Sparkling Wine* producers. The process of making this premier wine is extremely interesting and should not be missed.

WHAT'S IN A LABEL?

What does the label on a bottle of Napa Valley Wine tell us? The label usually lists four items; the name of the winery, the grape(s) used in the wine, and the vintage year (when the grapes were picked). The fourth is a little tricky. The label will either have the words *Estate Bottled*, *Reserve*, or neither listed. Let's examine these terms to see what they mean. In this manner, when serving a bottle of premium Napa Valley wine at your next dinner party, you can really impress your friends with your newfound knowledge.

Name of Winery

The name of the winery is obvious, although a different approach is used by many other countries. For example, the French designate their wines by regions such as *Bordeaux* or *Burgundy*.

Name of Wine / Grape(s) used to produce the Wine

This could be Cabernet Sauvignon, Pinot Noir, Merlot, Zinfandel, or another variety. However, some wineries blend different grapes to produce a special wine. For example, a winemaker may develop a wine blending a certain percentage of Cabernet, Merlot, and a small amount of another grape. In this instance, the wine may have a special unique name. American premium wines also have a label on the back usually listing the percentage of each grape used. In addition, the label may highlight the particular vineyard or *Appellation* where the grapes were grown. Lastly, in order for a wine to be listed as a *Napa Valley Wine*, the majority of grapes used to produce the wine must have been grown in the Napa Valley.

Vintage Year

The *Vintage Year* will also be noted. The year is not the year of release, rather it's the year the grapes were harvested and crushed. For example, the date on the label may be 2003, but the wine may not have been released to the public for sale until 2005. Wine needs to age over time, red wine taking a bit longer than white.

Estate / Estate Bottled

Estate / Estate Bottled simply means the winery harvests grapes from its own vineyards, processes the wine, and bottles at its main facility. Oddly enough, not all wineries own vineyards. Many purchase premium grapes from land owners in the vicinity. In this case, since the winery doesn't own the vineyard, it apparently can't use the term *Estate / Estate Bottled* on their label.

Reserve / Private Reserve

You'll also see the word *Reserve* or *Private Reserve* on some bottles of Napa Valley wines. This is usually the winery's flagship release, the cream of the crop. The winery may have used grapes from a select vineyard, or produced a limited quantity of wine from a spectacular harvest. In any event, it's the best the winery produces. *What if the label says Reserve but doesn't say Estate Bottled?* In this case, the winery probably purchased premier grapes from a nearby land owner.

Let's say the label has the name of the winery and the word *Merlot or Chardonnay* on it, but doesn't have the words *Estate* or *Reserve*. By now, you should have no problem figuring this one out.

At this point, I think you've got the hang of it. In most cases, you'll have little trouble reading premium wine labels. It's actually quite simple once you understand the terms we've defined. If your just starting to explore the world of fine wines, here's an idea. Go on an expedition to your local wine shop and check out the Napa Valley wines on the rack. With the knowledge you've gained, try reading the labels. You'll be pleasantly surprised at just how much you've learned. It will also give you a leg up prior to your visit.

How is wine bottled?

A truly unique phenomenon occurs during bottling time. Many visitors expect to walk into a winery at any time and see wine being processed and bottled. Actually, there are very few wineries that have bottling plants. Only certain facilities can afford such technology or even have room for such a plant. However, all wineries must bottle their wine. *So how do they do it?* Interestingly enough, there are large trucks that have complete miniature bottling plants within the truck itself. When ready to bottle, a winery simply calls the company and a truck is sent to the facility to bottle on the premises. The wine is pumped into the truck and the process begins. It's a fascinating operation to watch. If you have a winery in mind, call and ask when they might be bottling. If occurring during your visit, they may allow you to observe.

Pairing

On the back label, some wineries list what foods might be best *paired* with the wine. For example, the label on a bottle of Merlot might suggest *"enjoy this wine with filet mignon, rack of lamb, or chicken braised in red wine."* Don't forget to check the label on the back. It may help you decide what foods to serve with the wine you're considering.

THE LABEL IS ONLY A GUIDE
TO WHAT'S IN THE BOTTLE

If you don't remember anything else, remember this. *The label is only a "guide."* Walk into any premium wine shop in the country and you'll notice one thing, beautiful wine labels. As an artist, I enjoy browsing through the racks looking at labels. The artwork, colors, and designs are fascinating. Wineries spend big bucks on label design. After all, the label is the first thing we see on the bottle. I've actually bought a bottle of wine because I liked the label. The wine business is very competitive and advertising is a big part of it. What better way to get one's attention than to catch your eye with a provocative label.

Before we continue to the next section, allow me to share an experience I had not long ago. I was invited to a *label tasting* party at a friends house. There must have been ten different *wine labels* on the table, some very striking. We tasted labels the better part of the evening, but in the end they all tasted about the same. Sound a bit crazy? Of course it does, but I think you get the point. The label doesn't tell us what the wine will taste like. *But how will I know what the wine tastes like unless I buy it?* That's why your planning your trip to the Napa Valley, not just to visit wineries, but to *taste wine.* This way, you'll have a fair idea of what might be in that next bottle of XYZ Napa Valley Cabernet you decide to purchase. However, there are other alternatives, and we'll cover them shortly. *But, I don't know how to taste wine! How is it done? What am I looking for?* We'll also answer these questions and more in the following section, *The "Art of Wine Tasting" - How to Taste Wine.*

Part 7

The "Art of Wine Tasting" How to Taste Wine

Initially, the process of tasting wine may seem confusing. *How is it done? Is there a special technique? What am I looking for? How do I know if a wine is good, bad, or otherwise? Do I swallow it ... spit it out ... roll it in my mouth?* Many believe there's some magical technique to wine tasting, some mysterious process known only to sophisticated wine connoisseurs. Actually, the process isn't complicated at all. In a moment, we'll examine some basic wine tasting fundamentals. But first, a few words of advice.

NEVER BEGIN YOUR DAY TASTING WINE ON AN EMPTY STOMACH. Have a good breakfast before starting your day. *But I rarely have breakfast, coffee's enough for me!* At least have something, even if it's a bagel. It's not a good idea to start out tasting wine on an empty stomach, even if it is the best wine in the world. Remember, I've conducted hundreds of wine tours. Trust me on this one.

In addition, remember another thing. Everyone's palate (that thing in our mouths that discerns tastes) is different. What I might like in a wine, you may not. So begin with this premise. *IF YOU DON'T LIKE IT, DON'T DRINK IT!*

OK, you're ready to begin your day. But before you walk into that first winery, here's another point to be aware of. At times, the hospitality agent at the facility you're about to enter may attempt to convince you their wine is the best thing going ... and it may well be. Wineries are in business to sell wine, and the business is very competitive. So be ready for this. However, most wineries in the area are very respectful of their local competition. There's a professionalism and camaraderie in the wine business not found in many other industries. Often, a tasting room agent may even recommend another winery down the road for a specific variety. On the other hand, don't allow others to convince you of a wine's quality. Although they may have a point in their presentation, you be the final judge. *If you don't like it, don't drink it!*

Appearance of the Wine

Hold your glass by the stem rather than the bowl. In this manner, any heat in your hand will not be transferred to the glass. Observe the color of the wine. Each wine has its own unique color. *Swirl* the wine in the glass. Some wines form *legs*, the fluid that slowly runs down the glass after *swirling* the wine. Is the wine clear or cloudy? Premium wines are usually pristine and rich in color. Observe how the light filters through the wine. Look at that bright thin layer just at the surface. In wine terms, it's called the *meniscus*. Anyone who has ever had arthroscopic knee surgery will recognize this term.

Swirling and Sniffing the Wine

Here's a *swirling technique* that will show your friends just how sophisticated you really are. You can practice this before your visit. Put some water or another liquid in a wine glass, filling it about half way. Place it on a table … preferably a wooden table. Put the stem between your index and middle fingers, then press down lightly on the base. With the palm of your hand resting on the table, begin spinning the base around, applying enough pressure to keep the base stable. The liquid will begin to *swirl*. Try this technique when you first step up to a winery tasting counter. You'll look like a real pro!

Now that you're a pro at *swirling*, swirl a glass of wine. By doing so, your mixing air with the wine. Smell the wine. *What do you smell? What aromas do you sense?* A wine's aroma is referred to as it's "*bouquet*" or "*nose.*" Most premium wines smell very fresh. Bad wines may have a moldy smell. The aromas associated with wines may include fruits, earthy smells, chocolate, and many others.

Tasting the wine

As noted, each person's palate is different. This explains why people prefer different wines. So let's begin with some basics. You can practice these techniques at home before your visit, or do it when you arrive at your first winery. Take a sip of wine. Swish it around in your mouth. If you don't like it, spit it out. This is allowed at tasting counters where receptacles are provided. If you like it, swallow it. Notice the different sensations in your mouth. Different parts of your mouth react with varying sensations. You may sense bitterness, sweetness, a sour taste, or even an acid sensation. *What do these sensations represent?* First, *sweetness* is usually detected by the tip of your tongue. A dry wine is the opposite of a sweet wine. *Is the wine sweet or dry?* Notice the *tannin* taste in the wine. *Tannins* are compounds that are part of the grape skins. They are higher in red wines because the grapes are processed with their skins on. A significant amount of *tannin* in a wine may cause it to be either strong or bitter. Less *tannin* generally yields a softer taste.

Great wine or not so great?

Generally, wines produced in the premium wine regions of the world are of the highest quality. However, some may not agree with us. Some may just taste bad to us. Remember, each person's palate is different. It basically comes down to your own personal taste. A *Johannesburg Riesling* may suit your palate better than a *Chardonnay*. These two wines are processed from different varieties of white grapes. However, you may like one and be indifferent to the other, pointing out the importance of tasting the wine. In addition, a *Cabernet* from two separate wineries may taste different. Same grape, different vintners. *Why is this?* It may relate to the geographical area the grapes came from, the different philosophies of the winemakers, or possibly how the wine was processed. Again, the importance of *tasting the wine*.

There may be a few lessor quality wines produced in the premium wine regions of the world. However, it's usually not the wine that's inferior. Rather, it may have been something that went wrong inside the bottle after it was corked. A faulty corking process may have allowed compounds to enter, deteriorating the wine. So smell the cork. If it's moldy or smells bad, chances are the wine may have been affected. Recently, many wineries have changed from corks to other methods of sealing bottles. Apparently, these efforts have been introduced to prevent wine damage or are simply just more economical.

Lastly, you might ask, *How can I taste a wine to judge its quality if it hasn't been opened yet? I can't visit the Wine Country every month!* Great point. However, there's an answer. Most premium wine shops offer weekly wine tastings. Check with them to ascertain what wines they may be offering. In addition, suggest they obtain wines you would like to taste. Another option is to have your own *Home Wine Tasting Party.* Invite your friends over and have them each bring a bottle of their favorite wine. This is a great way to sample wines you may have never tried.

Here's another unique idea. Have a *"Secret" Wine Tasting Party.* Tell your friends to bring a couple bottles of wine to the party. Before arriving, make sure they wrap each bottle in a brown paper bag, concealing their identity. Leave the bottle top visible so it can be opened. If the bottleneck has a foiled label containing the name of the winery, remove it. Now, label the paper bags with a number, beginning with 1,2,3, and so on. Before starting, open the bottles and let them *breath* for a short period, but don't remove the paper bag. Have everyone sample each wine, using the methods learned here. Make sure each person has a pen, listing the wines they liked the best, i.e., numbers 1, 3, 6, etc. In addition, have each participant list the reasons for their choices. Once the tasting is complete, unbag the bottles. You might be surprised to find out what you really like!

Wine Rating Scales

Often, upon release, a recognized *"Wine Expert"* may choose to sample a wine, assigning it a rating based upon their interpretation of quality. Ratings usually range from 70 to 100, but can be lower. A rating of 95 to 100 is considered outstanding, but rarely does a wine receive a rating of 100. Many premium wine shops list such ratings on each wine. The ratings can at least provide a guideline to quality when purchasing wine. In addition, several recognized wine magazines also list wine ratings.

Check out the following resources to obtain wine ratings plus a host of other information. They were current at the time of publication. The *Wine Enthusiast* magazine can be purchased on line at *www.*

wineenthusiast.com. Other sites include *www.winebusiness.com., www. winecountrythisweek.com.*, and *www.wine-searchers.com.*

Talk about technology, how about this alternative for obtaining wine ratings. Recently, I went to the *www.winebusiness.com* web site and punched in the key word *ratings*. Several sites came up. However, one was especially interesting. Wine ratings are *going mobile!* There are actually miniature computer programs and devices being produced that will provide the latest wine ratings at the touch of your finger. Quite innovative. But ... you've still gotta taste it to see if you like it!

The Final Results

Taste it first ... if you don't like it ... don't drink it.

© Goosecross Winery

Vintage Napa Valley Chardonnay

Part 8

Let's get started...
How to "Plan your Day"

Small, Medium, Large Wineries

Generally, wineries fall into three categories. Small, medium, and large. Seems simple, but that's about how it works. A winery's size in the industry is usually determined by how much wine, or rather how many *"cases of wine"* it normally produces annually. However, don't confuse size with quality. Most facilities produce outstanding vintages.

Routes to consider once in the Napa Valley

As noted earlier, the two main routes in the area are *Highway 29* on the western side and the *Silverado Trail* on the eastern side. Wineries are located all along these routes. *Highway 29* goes through the towns of *Napa, Yountville, Oakville, Rutherford, St. Helena,* and *Calistoga.* It is the most traveled and can become congested in season, especially on weekends. The more rural *Silverado Trail* offers visitors a beautiful country ride through vineyard panoramas and is not as busy as *Highway 29.*

Well known facilities along *Highway 29* include *Domaine Chandon, Robert Mondavi, Cakebread, Rubicon Estate, Beaulieu, Sutter Home, Beringer* and *Charles Krug.* Wineries along the *Silverado Trail* include *Clos Du Val, Stags Leap, Mumm Napa Valley, Rutherford Hill, Joseph Phelps,* and *Sterling Vineyards,* but there are many others.

If you plan your day well, you should be able to visit 5 to 6 wineries. Tasting wine at each facility takes only about 20 minutes or so at most. If you've laid out your itinerary in advance, you can easily visit this many without rushing … including lunch.

If you decide to tour along the *Silverado Trail*, you'll avoid a fair amount of traffic. However, don't eliminate wineries along *Highway 29*. If your in on a weekend and choose to tour along *Highway 29*, begin your day AT THE TOP OF THE NAPA VALLEY, visiting wineries from NORTH TO SOUTH. Start by driving up the *Silverado Trail* around 9:30 a.m., then cross over to *Highway 29* and work your way *"down the valley."* You can cross over to *Highway 29* at any number of points in the north, including Deer Park Road, Bale Lane, or Dunaweal Lane. You can also drive to the very top of the valley and cross over in Calistoga on Lincoln Avenue. It just depends on the places you desire to visit along *Highway 29*. It's a short drive up no matter where you start from. Try following this plan in season and especially on weekends. By doing so, you'll avoid the larger crowds coming up *Highway 29* early in the day. Most will be visiting wineries in the usual manner, SOUTH TO NORTH. By going NORTH TO SOUTH, you'll be moving against the heavier traffic coming up the valley, eventually ending your day in the lower valley. There will be a certain amount of congestion no matter where your at, but if the majority of wineries you choose are on *Highway 29*, this plan will work best.

If touring on a weekday or even a weekend during the slower months, visiting wineries in the usual manner from SOUTH TO NORTH won't pose a problem, especially if you've planned ahead. However, I've always enjoyed beginning many of my tours at the top of the valley. If you can time it right, there's something special about being the first at a winery to taste that great Cabernet that was just uncorked.

Days of the week

Your probably tired of hearing this by now, but try to visit between *Monday and Thursday*. If a weekend is your only alternative, begin early. Remember, the region gets an influx of traffic from Bay Area visitors on weekends. If not staying in the Napa Valley, plan to arrive no later than 9:00 a.m. This gives you plenty of time to relax and get ready for the day. I've always felt the best days to visit were either *Tuesday or*

Wednesday. I also realize you must adhere to your own schedule and specific days to visit. In this regard, throughout the book I'll share additional time saving suggestions no matter when your visiting.

© Goosecross Winery

Winetasting at Goosecross

Part 9

Visiting the Wineries ... What to Expect

Most wineries are open all year, including some major holidays. However, if visiting on a holiday, call ahead to make sure. Wineries open around 10:00 a.m. and close about 4:30 p.m. *Public Wineries* are open on a walk-in basis and don't require appointments. *Private Wineries* are divided into two categories; those not open to the public and those open but requiring advance reservations.

VISITING THE WINERIES
Appointments Required? ... Public or Private Winery?

Most *Tour Maps* indicate if wineries are *Public* or *Private*. In addition, they list hours of operation, phone numbers, and other valuable information. Prior to your visit, obtain a current *Winery Tour Map* and use it to plan your visit. It will save a lot of time and hassle. Visit *www. napavalleytourmap.com* to purchase one, or contact any of the local Chambers of Commerce for free information. As indicated earlier, I produce a locally endorsed *Winery Map* used by thousands of visitors to the area. It is updated annually and easy to read. However, no matter where you obtain this information, get it prior to your trip. You won't be sorry.

As noted, many *Private* wineries are open to the public, but require appointments in advance. *Public* wineries don't require appointments. You merely walk in during regular business hours and are served. However, REMEMBER THE FOLLOWING POINT WHEN VISITING "PUBLIC" WINERIES ON WEEKENDS IN SEASON ... ALWAYS

CONSIDER CALLING IN ADVANCE OF YOUR ARRIVAL, ESPECIALLY IF VISITING A SMALLER FACILITY. Many a first time visitor has walked into a small *Public Winery* expecting to pony up to the tasting bar and be served … only to find a room packed with people where one sweet hospitality agent is attempting to pour wine, explain the history of the winery, and at the same time deal with the guy who has already had his limit. If only in for a brief visit, why waste time driving to a winery, then walking in only to find you'll be standing in a long line. Your time is more valuable, so let's explore a better way to do it. It takes a little effort, but will save tons of wasted time.

Here's the idea. Your driving along to your next stop. The person next to you has a good winery map at hand. Get the tasting room phone number off the map and have them call ahead with their cell phone. *Is the tasting room crowded? Any problem getting served?* In most cases, there won't be a problem. However, this small effort will save a lot of time and frustration, especially during the summer months and on weekends. In addition, there's another situation that occurs on weekends, one that can cause additional frustration. It's called a winery *Special Event.*

On occasion, a winery may be conducting a *Special Event.* These usually occur on weekends and are *closed to the public.* They include parties for *Wine Club* members, weddings, plus other affairs. For the typical visitor, there's no way of knowing in advance if such events are occurring other than calling ahead. Well, there is one other way. You can always drive to the winery expecting to taste some great wine, only to find a sign blocking the entrance, *Sorry for the inconvenience, winery closed today!* Why waste time when a simple phone call does the trick. By calling ahead, you'll be aware of a possible inconvenience and can easily adjust your itinerary. Better yet, call the wineries you intend to visit well in advance of your trip. You'll know if a *Special Event* is scheduled and can simply substitute another located in the same geographical area.

One last point about calling ahead. If planning to visit with a group of 6 or more, *always call ahead for an appointment.* Most wineries have no problem designating a special hospitality agent to such a group, as long as an advance reservation is made.

TASTING FEES

Although some wineries offer complimentary tasting, most charge a fee. Years ago, tasting was complimentary. I remember the first winery in the Napa Valley that began charging. It was about $2.00, and was implemented to recoup losses resulting in patrons walking away with wine glasses used for tasting. However, another phenomenon eventually occurred that more readily influenced wineries to begin charging. As the region became more popular, many visitors came to only *"taste wine,"* having no thought of purchasing wine. Eventually, wineries began charging a nominal fee to offset losses in the large amounts of wine being poured. However, many wineries do make a serious attempt at reimbursing patrons in other ways. Be sure to ask if the winery will *credit back* the tasting fee toward a wine purchase. Many offer this service. In addition, some allow couples to *share a taste*, where only one fee is required. Still others allow visitors to keep the logo wine glass used for tasting.

Tasting fees can vary depending upon the wines tasted. At the time of publication, fees averaged about $10.00 per person, and usually included three selected wines. However, fees can be higher if tasting more exclusive *Reserve* or *Limited Edition Wines*.

At times, a winery may also offer *complimentary tasting coupons*. The coupons might be for a single tasting, a tasting for two, or buy one tasting … get the second free. Contact the local Chambers or Visitors Bureaus to see if they have any. If so, suggest sending a SASE. They might just mail them to you. In addition, there are many wine magazines available to the public. They can usually be obtained from the same sources, or check the *Directory* in the back of the book. Wineries often advertise in these magazines. At times, a winery ad will include a *Tear Out* that provides a *two for one tasting* … or even a *full complimentary tasting for two.*

Lastly, consider calling ahead to verify the tasting fees at the wineries you intend to visit, especially if your on a tight budget. In this manner, you'll avoid any unpleasant surprises when you arrive. The winery may even offer you some complimentary tasting coupons if available. Don't forget to ask about this. Remember, the wineries want your business. If such coupons are available, they may even mail them to you. Offer to send a SASE for their convenience. It might work!

Exclusive *"Private Tastings"*

Many wineries offer *Exclusive Private Tasting Programs*. They're usually held in beautiful surroundings and always require a reservation. It's simply a matter of contacting the winery in advance to make the arrangements. *Private* facilities usually welcome the opportunity to cater to a small group interested in trying their wines. Often, the wines will be paired with food appropriate to the occasion. Fees for such events can vary, depending upon the wines tasted and food served. If you have a winery in mind, call to see if they have such a program. But remember, call well in advance … and I don't mean one or two weeks. Try one or two months or even longer! Other knowledgeable visitors are aware of such programs and time slots can book up early.

TAKING A TOUR

Guided Winery Tours

I suggest you take at least one *Guided Winery Tour* during your stay. You can visit a winery offering *Public Tours* where no appointment is necessary, or one that is *Private* requiring an appointment. Wineries offering *Guided Tours* usually have specific schedules for their tours. They may be conducted every hour, once per day, or possibly three times a day. Check your winery tour map for those facilities offering such tours and if they require an appointment. The *Ten Sample Tours* listed in *Part 12* contain at least one *Guided Tour* in each itinerary.

Guided Tours usually last about an hour and can be very educational. In many cases, depending upon the weather, you'll not only go through the facility, but may walk through the vineyards as well. Wine tasting is usually conducted at the end. One *Guided Tour* per day is adequate, spending the balance of the day tasting wine at other facilities in the area.

Bus Tours, Private Tour Companies

What if I'm staying in the Bay Area, but don't feel like driving to the Napa Valley? Are there any companies that provide Bus Tours to the region? Yes, there are several. Go on line to *www.sanfrancisco.com* and do a search for *Napa Valley Tours*. You can also try *www.inetours.com*, current at the time of publication. *What if I'm staying in the Napa Valley, would rather not drive, but would still like to go on a Group Tour? Any options for me?* Absolutely. Check out the Napa web site at *www.napavalley.com*. and find the *tours category.* You'll find several bus companies offering this service. They'll pick you up at your hotel, then you'll join others for a day touring the region. Most hotels in the area can set everything up for you. Lastly, there are some great *Limo Tour Companies* offering *Private Tours* as well.

The advantages of the larger *Bus Tours* are obvious. You don't need to drive or plan your day, you're with other people on the bus, and the price is affordable. It can also be quite relaxing sitting back watching the vineyard panoramas pass by while someone else deals with the traffic. A good way to go. However, there are a couple disadvantages. First, only certain wineries in the area provide parking for the larger buses. In this regard, there are some restrictions on the wineries you'll be visiting. Secondly, tour buses are usually on a set schedule, restricting you to being on the bus according to their time table. There may be other disadvantages; however, bus tours offer a very relaxing alternative for many visitors.

How about a "Private" Tour where someone else does the driving and arranges everything? Or, what about my company or organization? Can a "Private" Tour be set up for us? Yes, there are several companies in the area offering such programs. Go to the Napa web site, find the *Tours* link, then check out the various services available. *"Private" Tours* can be expensive, but meet the needs of those looking for that special attention.

TOUR FEES

Tour Fee's - Public Wineries

Tour fees at *Public* wineries can vary from about $10.00 per person to approximately $25.00 or more, depending upon the facility visited and the wines tasted. Tours last about an hour, but can go longer. Look through your winery map for those *Public* facilities offering *Guided Tours.*

Tour Fees - Private Wineries

Tour fees at *Private Wineries* can also vary. The best advice is to check your tour map for wineries offering tours by appointment, then call to check on the fees. In addition, don't let the word *Private* prevent you from contacting the winery. If it conducts tours, but requires an appointment, all this means is they don't want visitors showing up unannounced. They may also limit their tours to a certain number of people during specific times of the day. This can be an advantage because the group will be smaller than those visiting larger *Public* wineries. It's not unusual for groups of 25, 30, or more to attend tours at the larger popular facilities. Whereas, a *Private Tour* at a smaller winery may only have 8 to 10 people or less. In this case, the tour is more personal, giving one a chance to ask questions. So seriously consider the smaller *Private* wineries when desiring a *Guided Tour.*

Tour Fees - "Self Guided Tours" - Public Wineries

Some *Public* wineries offer *Self Guided Tours*. You simply pay a nominal admission fee that usually includes wine tasting. Upon entering, you'll follow a designated route through the facility at your own pace. These tours are especially enjoyable if your looking for a less structured alternative. Check your winery map for facilities offering such tours. The *Ten Sample Day Tours* in *Part 12* include at least two wineries offering *Self Guided Tours*.

WINERY "CAVE TOURS"

Many facilities store their wine in caves. The temperature is relatively constant year round, providing the perfect environment for wines to age. As part of a *Guided Tour*, the winery usually includes a walk through the caves. It's a unique experience and especially enjoyable on a hot summers day. Sound scary? Don't worry, we're not talking about Dracula's summer vacation home here. Most caves have been manually dug and are very safe. In fact, many have sections that are heated and dedicated exclusively to private wine parties, luncheons, and dinners. If your planning a group visit to the area, contact the winery your interested in to see if they offer such programs. Ask how to arrange a catered luncheon or dinner event. This is a *Napa Valley Experience* you'll never forget. One thing to remember though. Most facilities offering such programs require a minimum group number. However, this is a great alternative for corporate events, meetings, or business seminars. Over the years, I've arranged many such events for groups from around the country. They were always a big hit. But check well in advance. By now, you should know what *Well in Advance* means.

PURCHASING WINE

Usually, one can purchase wine at the facility visited. In most cases, they'll ship directly to your address. However, shipping charges can be expensive, so be ready for this. In addition, there are direct mail outlets in the area that specialize in shipping wine. They have special wine boxes in stock for just such requests.

WINE CLUBS

Many facilities also have their own *Wine Clubs*. Information on such clubs can be obtained by contacting the winery directly or by going to their web site. Once a member, you'll be contacted about *Special Programs* offered. The winery may even ship new wine releases to you on a regular basis. You'll have to pay for the wine, but will no doubt receive a membership discount. In addition, there are other advantages. A winery may also conduct *Special Events* throughout the year for its members. Joining a *Wine Club* is a great way to try out new releases and become familiar with the winery and it's programs.

BUYING WINE BEFORE RELEASED

At times, wine can be purchased similar to the futures market in commodities. Wine must age over time prior to release. A winery's reputation for outstanding limited vintages may be so high that upon release its wine could sell out immediately. In this regard, some facilities offer clients the opportunity to purchase wine on what might be considered a *futures* basis, while the wine is still aging in the barrel. Basically, the buyer is wagering the winery will produce another superb vintage. Thus, the buyer has already committed to the purchase and should be assured of delivery upon release. If your interested in a particular winery, ask if they have such a program.

Part 10

Restaurants - Picnics - Winery Events

RESTAURANTS

The Napa Valley has some of the finest dining establishments in the world. We can't list them all here. However, several will be noted with a geographical reference for the towns of *Napa, Yountville, Oakville, Rutherford, St. Helena, and Calistoga.* This is not an endorsement of one over another. For a complete list of restaurant's and cuisine's offered, go to *www.napavalley.com.,* click on the town of your choice, then the key word *dining.* The following information was accurate at the time of publication.

Napa

Consider visiting **COPIA**, - *500 First Street - 707-259-1600.* The 60,000 square foot center was built under the direction of vintner Robert Mondavi and is oriented to wine, food, and the arts. The center has two options for dining. The first is a wonderful delicatessen, **The American Market Cafe**. The second is the upscale restaurant, **Julia's Kitchen** - *707-265-5700,* fashioned after the famous patron saint of the pantry, *Julia Child.* It offers marvelous California Wine Country cuisine. Reservations always required.

Another alternative on the outskirts of Napa is the **Royal Oak Restaurant** at *Silverado Resort - 1600 Atlas Peak Road -707-257-0200.* The Royal Oak offers classic steakhouse cuisine in beautiful resort surroundings.

The **Napa Valley Wine Train** is another outstanding choice if you've got the time - *1275 McKinstry Street - 707-253-2111.* The train ride provides brunch, lunch, and dinner excursions. Reservations always required.

Yountville

The quaint resort town of Yountville provides numerous dining alternatives. An old favorite is the **Napa Valley Grill** - *Highway 29 and Madison Street - 707-944-8686*, offering California cuisine. Some vineyard views.

Located next to **Vintage 1870**, *6525 Washington Street*, is **Pacific Blues Cafe** - *6525 Washington Street - 707-944-4455*, a laid back casual restaurant with limited seating inside and out. Just north of Vintage 1870 is **Compadres Mexican Bar & Grill** - *6539 Washington Street - 707-944-2406*, another favorite with the locals.

The **Lakeside Grill** - *7901 Solano Avenue -707-944-2426*, is located at the Yountville Golf Course. Seating inside or out at this casual restaurant. Outside seating offers beautiful views looking west toward the Mayacaymus Mountains. Outstanding food, great scenery, and affordable.

The **Restaurant at Domaine Chandon Winery** - *1 California Drive - 707-944-2892* is one of the finest dining experiences in the Napa Valley. Reservations always required, plus a casual dress code. The restaurant is closed on Tuesdays and Wednesdays. The **French Laundry** - *6640 Washington Street - 707-944-2380*, has long been known as one of the finest upscale dining establishments in the world. Outstanding cuisine. Reservations difficult to obtain and usually booked months in advance. One of the few Napa Valley establishments requiring a strict dress code.

Just up the road from Yountville is **Brix** - *7377 St. Helena Highway - 707-944-2749*, offering California cuisine plus views of the surrounding hills from most tables.

Another long time favorite among locals and visitors is **Mustards Grill** - *7399 St. Helena Highway - 707-944-2424*. Reservations always required.

Check out the above restaurants and others on the Yountville web site at *www.yountville.com*

Oakville / Rutherford

One of the more popular restaurants in the valley is **The Rutherford Grill** - *1180 Rutherford Road - 707-963-1792*. The Grill offers outstanding California style dining on a first come first served basis.

Then there's the famous **Oakville Grocery** - *7856 St. Helena Highway - 707-944-8802*, an old grocery store located along *Highway 29* offering a gourmet delicatessen, picnic box lunches, and just about everything else you might desire for a quick snack. A really fun place to visit.

For the discerning diner, consider **Auberge du Soleil** - *180 Rutherford Hill Road - 707-963-1211*, on the eastern side of the valley. This beautiful hillside retreat is half way up *Rutherford Hill Road* off the rural *Silverado Trail*. The views of the valley floor are breathtaking. Excellent mediterranean style French influenced cuisine. Reservations required.

St. Helena

St. Helena also has many options to choose from. For a great burger or sandwich, try **Taylor's Refresher** - *933 Main Street - 707-963-3486*. An old favorite, **Taylor's** is located on *Highway 29* at the southern entrance to St. Helena, *Taylor's* has picnic tables for your convenience. But remember, if your stopping on a weekend in season, be prepared for lines. Consider calling in your order ahead.

Two other outstanding restaurants at the southern end of the city are **Martini House**, *1245 Spring Street - 707-963-2233* and **Tra Vigne** - *1050 Charter Oak Avenue - 707-963-4444*.

The **Culinary Institute of America**, or *"CIA"* is located at the north end of the city. Future chefs train here in a variety of disciplines. The *"CIA"* is housed in the old *Christian Brother's Greystone* winery building, a massive stone structure worth visiting. The **Wine Spectator Greystone Restaurant** is located on the premises. This is a dining experience one should seriously consider. The environment is stunning. Guests can also observe the chefs working feverishly over the gourmet meals. Inside seating plus patio dining with outstanding vineyard views from the terrace. *2555 Main Street, 707-967-1010*.

Calistoga

The small western style town of Calistoga is the northern most community in the Napa Valley. Famous for its hot springs and mud baths, it too offers outstanding dining opportunities. Most of the restaurants are located on Lincoln Avenue, the main street going through town. Go on line and check out what's available.

Brannan's Grill - *1374 Lincoln Avenue - 707-942-2233*, is a local favorite, offering American cuisine. **The Calistoga Inn** - *1250 Lincoln*

Avenue - 707-942-4101, is another favorite with outdoor seating under an arbor.

The Wappo Bar & Grill Bistro - *1226 Washington Street - 707-942-4712*, is just off Lincoln Avenue. During the summer months, guests can sit outside in the patio and dine under a grape arbor.

The Cal Mart Deli at *1491 Lincoln Avenue - 707-942-9686*, is a good place to get a quick snack all the way up to a gourmet box lunch.

PICNICS & PICNIC FACILITIES

Picnics

How about a picnic with wine on a beautiful day in the Napa Valley? Sounds pretty good huh? Weather permitting, there are plenty of opportunities for picnics in the area. All you need is a little direction.

Here's a great idea. *Prepare your picnic lunch the night before.* Buy a cheap styrofoam cooler, fill it with ice and goodies, then take off for your Wine Country tour the next morning. For lunch, stop by a winery picnic grounds and enjoy the fixings. Shortly, I'll share some picnic facilities you can use.

Located up and down the valley are delicatessens and markets that can fill your picnic needs easily. We've already mentioned a couple. Centrally located is the **Oakville Grocery** in Oakville, *707-944-8802*. **The Cal Mart Deli** is located in Calistoga at *1491 Lincoln Avenue - 707-942-9686*. There are also supermarkets in the major towns along the way. In addition, check out **Dean & Deluca** - *607 St. Helena Highway - 707-967-9980*, a gourmet food market located at the southern end of St. Helena across from *V. Sattui Winery.* Many of these deli's and markets prepare *Gourmet Box Picnic Lunches* for such occasions.

BUT REMEMBER THE FOLLOWING POINT WHEN PURCHASING PICNIC LUNCHES AT THE POPULAR DELI'S AND MARKETS THROUGHOUT THE VALLEY. Almost anyone would love to have a picnic lunch with a little wine on a beautiful Napa Valley day ... *wouldn't you agree?* So you're in for the weekend and decide to stop at one of the places I've mentioned. Can't wait to pick up a great box lunch; maybe some chilled wine, cheese, salami, french bread, whatever. Mmmmmm! You walk in and there's 10 people standing in line waiting to be served. Behind the counter one person is frantically preparing 10 gourmet box lunches! The deli's do make a valiant attempt to prepare enough in advance for the crowds, but I think you get the point. Do this instead. *CALL A DAY OR TWO IN ADVANCE AND ORDER YOUR LUNCHES. THEY'LL BE READY FOR YOU WHEN YOU ARRIVE.* You'll be informed of what's on the menu and can choose whatever you desire. Better yet, if you really want it easy, do what I've done for clients over the years. Call one of the deli's before your trip and have them *fax a menu.* Merely make your choices, put it on your credit card, and inform them when you'll be arriving to pick up your lunches. It takes a little planning, but the satisfaction of walking by lines of people waiting to be served makes the effort well worth it. You can then scoot off and enjoy the rest of the day. I hate waiting in lines ... who doesn't? I'll do anything I can within reason to avoid them. I suggest you adopt the same philosophy when visiting the area. It will pay dividends.

Picnic Facilities

Many wineries offer outstanding venues to enjoy your picnic. What better place to have lunch than at a winery picnic grove with a beautiful view of the vineyard's. Many are open to the public, but may require an advance reservation. *How does one find out where they're located?* The best source of information is a current *Napa Valley Tour Map.* It will usually list wineries with picnic grounds and whether appointments are required.

The following is a partial list of wineries having picnic facilities open to the public on a walk-up or appointment basis, current at the time of publication. Call ahead to confirm: *Alpha Omega - Amizetta - Catacula Lake - Chimney Rock - Clos Du Val - Cuvaison - Diamond Oaks - Folie a Deux - Frank Family - Graeser - Hall - Hans Fahden - Judd's Hill - Monticello - Nichelini - Pina - Pine Ridge - Prager - Regusci - Rutherford Grove - Rutherford Hill - Robert Sinskey - V. Sattui.*

How about a place where you can have it all? Located just south of St. Helena, *V. Sattui Winery - 1111 White Lane - 707-963-7774,* has an extensive gourmet delicatessen, award winning wines, a large gift shop, and a popular picnic grove. But be ready for the crowds, especially on weekends during the summer. If the picnic area is too crowded, take your lunch to another less crowded spot.

Two last points about the use of picnic areas. Always call ahead in case the facility is in use for a *Winery Special Event,* especially on weekends. Secondly, the wineries usually offer these facilities on a complimentary basis, so consider visiting the tasting room for a bottle of their wine to enjoy with your meal.

WINERY EVENTS

Often, wineries will also advertise *Special Events* open to the public for a nominal fee. For example, a winery may be having a weekend BBQ, or a well known chef coming in for a cooking demonstration. *How does one find out about these events?* Go on line to *www.napavalley. com*. Check out the various wineries to see if they have a yearly calendar of events. You can also call directly to see what is planned throughout the year.

The Oakville Grocery

Part 11

Other Things To Do ...
Plus Things for the Kids To Do

Mud Baths - Hot Mineral Springs - Spas - Massages

Besides visiting wineries and tasting wine, there are many other things to do in the area. Check out the town of *Calistoga* where you can enjoy the soothing medicinal effects of mud baths, hot mineral pools, or massages. The town has several hotel spas that provide these amenities, including *Dr. Wilkinson's Hot Springs Resort - 1507 Lincoln Avenue - 707-942-4102*, and the *Golden Haven Spa Hot Springs Resort -1713 Lake Street - 707-942-6793*.

Hot Air Balloon Rides

Another popular activity is a hot air balloon ride over the valley. This is a wonderful way to see vineyard panoramas and winery estates from a different perspective. Most companies operate throughout the year, weather permitting. Balloons also take off bright and early, so be prepared. The balloon baskets can carry a number of people, so you'll be paired with others. Upon returning from the ride, a champagne brunch usually awaits guests. Because these excursions end around 10:00 a.m., there's still plenty of time to enjoy a full day touring the area. However, *consider this important point when planning a hot air balloon ride.* Weather plays a major factor in determining if a balloon takes off or not. If too windy, balloon companies will not fly. But there's another phenomenon that may change things as well ... *FOG*. At times during the summer, morning fog drifts in from the Bay Area. The fog usually burns off by noon. However, balloons must take off well before this, and will not fly in heavy fog. If fog is a factor the morning of a flight, most balloon companies won't cancel their flights. Rather, guests may be bused to a distant area where there is no fog. The balloon ride will occur, but may not be over the Napa Valley. Balloon rides are very expensive. Frankly, if I couldn't take mine over the Napa Valley, I'd rather wait for a sunny day. So check out the weather. If heavy fog is coming in that morning, you might consider switching your flight to another day. Research the various Hot Air Balloon companies at *www. napavalley.com.*

Napa Valley Wine Train

Take a ride on the popular *Napa Valley Wine Train - 1275 McKinstry Street, Napa - 707-253-2111.* Book your reservations well in advance. The train offers lunch, brunch, and dinner excursions … plus other interesting programs. However, if your only in for a brief visit, this may not be the best choice. I believe short visits should be concentrated on touring by automobile, or at least having a tour company drive you around. Although the train does make limited stops, it is somewhat restrictive in that you must stay on it most of the time. In addition, it only travels one route up and down the Napa Valley. But if you've got the extra time, the *Wine Train* is a great alternative and a lot of fun. *www.winetrain.com*

Bike Rides

You can bring your own bicycle, or rent one. This can be a very relaxing way to tour the area. However, a word of caution. You're in the *"Wine"* country. People are *tasting wine … and they're driving!* So take care. *Highway 29* and the *Silverado Trail* are the two main roads going through the area. I suggest you limit your bike riding to the *Silverado Trail* and the roads trailing off of it. Too much traffic on *Highway 29.* Make sure to have a good map in your possession listing all roads. You can research bike rental companies on the Napa web site.

Golf

I've played all the courses in the Napa Valley and surrounding areas. Most can be found on the Napa Web site. Simply click on the *"things to do"* category, then scroll down to *Golf*. Championship courses open to the public include the *Napa Municipal Course - 707-255-4333*, and *Hiddenbrooke - 707-558-0330*, just over the hill between the towns of Vallejo and Fairfield. Private courses include *Silverado Resort - 707-257-0200 and Meadowood Resort - 707-963-3646*. One must stay at these resorts to play the courses. Another scenic layout is the *Vintners Golf Course in Yountville - 707-944-1992*. This nine hole course is affordable, offers beautiful scenery, can be easily walked, and is friendly to lady golfers. For those with only a brief time to spend, the *Vintners Course* has it all. You can have breakfast in the *Lakeside Grill* at the course, play nine holes after breakfast, and still have the better part of the day left to tour the area.

Old Faithful Geyser

Another alternative (especially if you have the kids along) is a visit to the famous *Old Faithful Geyser - 1299 Tubbs Lane, Calistoga - 707-942-6463*. There's a moderate fee, but worth the price if your looking for something different. The geyser is one of only three *Old Faithful's* in the world designated such because of its constant and predictable eruptions. The eruptions are natural and occur every 45 minutes, spewing scalding water from 60 to 100 feet in the air. *www.oldfaithfulgeyser.com*.

The Petrified Forest

The Petrified Forest - 4100 Petrified Forest Road, Calistoga - 707-942-6667, is located just north of Calistoga. It's easy to find and is one of the finest examples of a pliocene fossil forest in the world. The park is privately owned and has been since its first proprietor started an excavating project on the property in 1871. A small admission fee is charged, but worth it if your looking for an interesting alternative. Check it out at *www.petrifiedforest.org*.

Bothe - Napa Valley State Park

Bothe State Park is located in the heart of the Napa Valley. Camping areas are available for individuals and groups. The park offers hiking, picnic tables, and a swimming pool (pool open daily from mid June through Labor Day). The park is open all year. Check it out on the Napa web site.

Skyline Wilderness Park

Skyline Wilderness Park - 2201 Imola Avenue, Napa - 707-252-0481. This natural wilderness park has a beautiful wildflower garden, camping and picnic areas, plus RV sites. There are also several trails for hikers and mountain bikers.

Take a ride to the Coast

Let's say you've already spent a couple of days in the area, but are pretty much *"wine tasted out."* Here's an interesting alternative. *Take a ride to the coast?* It's just a little over an hour's drive from the Napa Valley. Consider driving through the town of *Petaluma* where the classic movie *American Graffiti* was filmed. Then drive straight over to *Bodega Bay* where the famous Alfred Hitchcock thriller *The Birds* was filmed. You can get a great seafood lunch, enjoy the ocean, then drive back through the beautiful *Russian River Valley*. Over the years, when my wife and I wanted to get away from Napa for a day, this was one of our favorite trips.

Bay Link Ferry to San Francisco

If you're staying in the area, this idea can be a lot of fun. The *Bay Link Ferry Terminal* is located in the town of *Vallejo*, about 25 minutes south of Napa. There's plenty of parking at the terminal. You can drive down, leave your car, then take the ferry across the bay to San Francisco. The ride takes about an hour and ultimately ends up at the *Ferry Building* near *Pier 39*. From there, it's about a twenty minute walk to *Fisherman's Wharf*. If you choose not to walk, you can take a cab or shuttle from the Ferry Building to just about anywhere in the city. Not far from Fisherman's Wharf is the *Cable Car Terminal*. A ride on a cable car is always a treat. Often, my wife and I would take the ferry over to San Francisco, have some wonderful clam chowder at the wharf, then take the ferry back to Vallejo in the late afternoon. Schedules to and from San Francisco run throughout the day. Tickets can be purchased at the terminal office in Vallejo. *www.baylinkferry.com. - 707-643-3779.*

Infineon Raceway

Infineon Raceway is one of the premier auto race courses in the country. Located just 30 minutes from Napa, several major events are held here throughout the year, including Nascar, drag races, and the Grand Prix of Sonoma. Check out these events if your an avid race fan. The raceway is located at *29355 Arnold Drive in Sonoma.* Their web site is *www.searspoint.com. 1-800-870 -RACE.*

Napa Valley Opera House

The *Napa Valley Opera House* is located at *1000 Main Street, Napa - 707-226-7372.* It showcases excellence in music and the performing arts for audiences of all ages, including world class musical theater, plays, chamber music, jazz, opera, dance and other family programs. *www.nvoh.org.*

Shopping

There are many fine shops throughout the Napa Valley. One of the best complexes is located in the town of *Yountville.* The *Vintage 1870* is a multi story brick building offering specialty shops, galleries, and a host of other shopping alternatives. Check it out at *www.vintage1870. com. - 707-944-2451.* You won't be disappointed!

More "Other Things" to do

Go to the Napa web site and click on *Things To Do.* You'll find categories such as *Sightseeing, Recreational Sports, Antiques, Nightlife, Attractions, Shopping, Parks & Recreation, The Arts, and an Events Calendar.*

THINGS FOR THE KIDS TO DO

In all my years conducting wine tours, I've never visited a winery offering specific activities for children or teenagers. Teens are welcome, but obviously can't taste wine. I have conducted a few tours where teens did accompany their parents. Frankly, most of them were bored stiff. Unless absolutely necessary, I would recommend against bringing your children along, especially if your coming for only a brief visit. However, I also realize there are instances where you may have no choice but to bring them along. If so, make sure they're old enough to be involved in activities on their own … or bring grandma along. Let's look at some activities in the area kids might enjoy.

Bike Rentals

There are several bike rental companies in the valley. However, if bike rides are in the plan for your children or teens, caution them to be extremely alert on Napa Valley roads. In addition, have them stay off of *Highway 29*, concentrating their riding on the off roads from the *Silverado Trail* or in the small towns along the way. The town of Calistoga would be a great place to ride bikes and hang out. The traffic moves slowly through town, it's off the main roads, and is much safer. Plus, there's plenty for them to do in town.

Marine World Theme Park

Another great option for young children and teens is *Marine World Theme Park* in Vallejo, just 25 minutes away. They can spend the entire day watching wildlife, riding waterways, playing games, riding the roller coaster, plus enjoy a myriad of other activities. If your bringing teens, there's also the option of dropping them in Napa. They could shop, go to a movie, or just hang out as teens do. Yountville is another town with plenty of shops to visit. However, my best recommendation would be *Marine World* in Vallejo. Most kids would love this popular theme park. Go on line and check it out at *www.marineworldvallejo. com. - 707-643-6722.*

PB & J's (Party, Bounce & Jump)

Here's a place most young children would thoroughly enjoy. It's *PB & J's, 849 Jackson Street, No. 4, Napa - 707-226-5867*. This facility has inflatable jumps, a sports arena, and an obstacle course. At the time of publication, it was also offering day care trips. An *Open Jump* play period is available during the week. *www.partyatpbjs.com.*

Jelly Belly Candy Company

Another fun place to visit is the *Jelly Belly Candy Company* in Fairfield, about 25 minutes from the Napa Valley. It's a great alternative for the whole family. The tour is free and everyone can observe the process of how *Jelly Bellies* are made, plus taste them as well. Their web site is *www.jellybelly.com. - 800-953-5592.*

Bay Link Ferry

Mentioned earlier, the *Bay Link Ferry* to San Francisco would be another option most kids and teens would thoroughly enjoy. There are many shops and activities near Fisherman's Wharf. Plenty for the kids to do. However, it would probably be best for an adult to accompany the kids on this type of outing.

Part 12

Ten "Sample Day Tours" Anyone Can Take

The *Wine Tours* listed here are ones you can easily take on your own. They include unique wineries offering beautiful atmospheres, world class wines, and diverse geographical venues. They're organized to avoid most crowds and major traffic. But before we begin, let's establish a game plan that will result in a more enjoyable visit.

Forgive me for stressing this again, but *always plan well in advance*. Once your ducks are lined up, you can simply show up and follow the itinerary chosen, but avoid the temptation to alter the itineraries. You'll thoroughly enjoy them just as they are.

There is one *Guided Tour* listed in most itineraries. If you recall, this is a tour where a winery guide person takes you and others through the facility. It usually takes about an hour. If an advance appointment is required, it will be noted. Don't wait too long to make the appointment. *Guided Tours* at *"private"* facilities can book up weeks in advance, especially on weekends and holidays. You'll need to show up for your *Guided Tour* about 15 minutes early. The rest of your day will be very flexible, visiting the remaining wineries on the list at your own pace. All phone numbers, addresses, and web sites have been listed as of the date of publication.

The tours are not listed in any specific order. Just choose the one that best appeals to you. Some begin in the north valley, some in the south, and some mid valley. If staying overnight in the area, you might feel obligated to choose a tour that begins in close proximity to your place of lodging. However, this is not necessary. The beginning points of each are within short driving distance from most spots in the Napa Valley.

When making your selection, be aware of this factor. At times, wineries schedule *Special Events*. As noted earlier, these include weddings, luncheons, or wine club parties. Most are scheduled on weekends. In addition, a tasting room may be unusually crowded on a given day. If your tour is on a weekend or holiday, make sure to have the tasting room phone numbers of the wineries on your list. Simply use your cell phone and call the winery on your tour shortly before arrival. In most cases, you'll have no problems getting in. However, a simple call will avoid wasting additional time, especially if a winery has scheduled a *Special Event* and is closed for the day. If your visit occurs on a weekend or holiday, you may even consider calling the wineries well in advance of your trip. This way, you'll know if an event is scheduled the day of your visit. If so, merely choose another within the same geographical area.

I've been on most of the tours listed here. Although it might seem difficult choosing one over another, you'll be delighted with any you select. But please avoid the temptation to switch the wineries around. They're organized geographically to help you experience the most from your day. In addition, you may notice the same winery listed in more than one tour. This was done for two reasons. First, the facility may be one I feel should be included more than once. Secondly, it probably fits in better geographically with others on the list.

For clarification, I'll repeat this point. With the exception of *Tour No. 10*, you'll need to make only one appointment for any given day. This will be at the facility where you'll have a *Guided Tour*. As noted above, the *Guided Tours* last about an hour and you must arrive 15 minutes early to register. The rest of your day will be very flexible, allowing anywhere from 20 to 30 minutes at each remaining winery on the list. If your visiting for more than a day, consider doing other tours on the list. In any event, throw your dart, choose a tour, start planning … and have a wonderful time!

SAMPLE DAY TOURS INCLUDED

Tour No. 1
Schramsberg, Lunch, Sterling, Dutch Henry, Rombauer, Rutherford Hill, Robert Sinskey.

Tour No. 2
Chateau Montelena, Lunch, Cuvaison, Ehlers Estate, Trinchero Family Estates, Prager Port Works & Winery, Sutter Home.

Tour No. 3
Raymond, Lunch, Duckhorn, Rombauer, Sterling Vineyards, Ehlers Estate, St. Clement Vineyards.

Tour No. 4
V. Sattui, Rutherford Hill, Lunch, Robert Sinskey, Regusci, Clos Du Val, Signorello, Darioush.

Tour No. 5
Monticello, Del Dotto Caves, Lunch, Reynolds Family, Regusci, Goosecross, Cliff Lede.

Tour No. 6
Hess Collection, Laird Family Estate, Lunch, Domaine Chandon, Diamond Oaks, Cliff Lede, Miner Family.

Tour No. 7
Hess Collection, Lunch, Andretti, Monticello, Trefethen, Domaine Chandon, Robert Mondavi.

Tour No. 8
Burgess, Rombauer, Ehlers Estate, Lunch, St. Clement, Markham, CIA - Culinary Institute of America.

Tour No. 9
Swanson Vineyards, Lunch, Beaulieu Vineyards, Caymus Vineyards, Conn Creek Winery, ZD Wines, Miner Family

Tour No. 10
Choose from the following two options depending upon the day of your visit:

Option No. 1 - Monday - Friday
Chappellet Vineyards, Lunch, Rustridge, Rutherford Hill

Option No. 2 - Saturday only
Kuleto, Lunch, Nichelini, Rustridge

Facilities in Tour No. 1
*Schramsberg, Sterling, Dutch Henry, Rombauer,
Rutherford Hill, Robert Sinskey*

Schramsberg Vineyards

Sterling Vineyards

Dutch Henry Winery

Rombauer Vineyards

Rutherford Hill Winery

Robert Sinskey Vineyards

Tour No. 1

North to South along Highway 29 and the Silverado Trail.
Most wineries will be located along the Silverado Trail.

Schramsberg, Lunch in Calistoga, Sterling Vineyards, Dutch Henry
Winery, Rombauer Vineyards, Rutherford Hill Winery, Robert Sinskey

Schramsberg Vineyards - *Guided Tour* - 10:00 a.m. to 11:30 a.m.
Phone No. - 707-942-4558 or 707-942-2414
Address - 1400 Schramsberg Road, Calistoga, California 94515
Web Site - www.schramsberg.com
Check web site for DIRECTIONS MAP
Appointment always required - Call well in advance
Cost per person - About $25.00. Well worth it!

Request the 10:00 a.m. tour. *Schramsberg* offers several tours throughout the day. If the 10:00 a.m. tour is booked, choose another and alter your remaining schedule for the rest of the day.

Schramsberg is a premier *Sparkling Wine* facility located just south of Calistoga. Take *Peterson Drive* west off *Highway 29*. Verify directions on the winery web site. You'll drive through a beautiful forest area up to the winery. *Schramsberg* became famous during the 70's when President Richard Nixon visited China on a goodwill tour. At that time, he presented *Schramsberg Sparkling Wine* to Chinese dignitaries. It turned out to be a big hit. The tour at *Schramsberg* lasts about an hour and one half. After touring the facility and its *Wine Caves*, you'll return to the tasting room to taste outstanding sparkling wine.

Lunch - 12:00 to 1:00 p.m.

After *Schramsberg*, drive into Calistoga for lunch. Check out the alternatives listed in *Part 10* or go on line to research your options. I like the *Calistoga Inn - 707-942-4101, Brannan's Grill - 707-942-2233*, and the funky *Wappo Bar & Bistro - 707-942-4712*. But, there are many others. You can also drop into the *Cal Mart Deli -1491 Lincoln Avenue - 707-942-9686*, for a deli sandwich or picnic lunch.

   * **Lunch on weekends** - If your in on a weekend, call ahead for lunch reservations. If up for a gourmet box lunch at the *Cal Mart Deli*, call a day or two ahead. They'll have it waiting when you arrive. This way, you'll avoid the weekend lines. After lunch, it's off for more wine tasting.

Sterling Vineyards - *Self Guided Tour* - 1:00 p.m. to 1:45 p.m.
Phone No. - 800-726-6136 or 707-942-3344
Address - 1111 Dunaweal Lane, Calistoga, California 94515
Web Site - www.sterlingvineyards.com
Tasting Fee - About $20.00 per person. Includes tram ride to winery.
No appointment required for wine tasting and Self Guided Tour

   Located south of Calistoga, *Sterling Vineyards* is a beautiful facility with outstanding views of the valley floor. It can get crowded on weekends, but worth the stop. You'll take a 7 minute tram ride to the top of the hill where the winery is located, then enjoy a *Self Guided* tour plus wine tasting.

Dutch Henry Winery - *Wine Tasting* - 2:00 p.m. to 2:30 p.m.
Phone No. - 888-224-5879 or 707-942-5771
Address - 4300 Silverado Trail North, Calistoga, California 94515
Web Site - www.dutchhenry.com
Tasting fee - $10.00 per person
No appointment required for wine tasting - 6 persons or less

   Dutch Henry is a small family owned winery along the rural *Silverado Trail*. The rustic tasting room is small, so call ahead to make sure you can get in. However, even if crowded in the summer, you can taste wine outside in the shade. A really fun place to visit.

Rombauer Vineyards - *Wine Tasting* - 2:45 p.m. to 3:15 p.m.
Phone No. - 707-967-5120
Address - 3522 Silverado Trail North, St. Helena, California 94574
Web Site - www.rombauer.com
Tasting fee - $10.00 per person
No appointment required for wine tasting - 6 persons or less

Always one of my favorite stops, *Rombauer* sits on a beautiful hillside with some views. Chardonnay is the signature wine produced here. The small tasting room can get a bit cramped on weekends, but there's usually plenty of staff to serve visitors. After *Rombauer*, head south down the *Silverado Trail* to your next stop, *Rutherford Hill Winery*.

Rutherford Hill Winery - *Wine Tasting* - 3:30 p.m. to 4:00 p.m.
Phone No. - 707-963-1871
Address - 200 Rutherford Hill Road, Rutherford, California 94573
Web Site - www.rutherfordhill.com
Tasting fee - $10.00 per person
No appointment required for wine tasting - 6 persons or less

Rutherford Hill Winery is located up *Rutherford Hill Road* off the *Silverado Trail*. The winery sits perched atop a hill with spectacular views. It was one of the first facilities in the region to begin producing premium Merlot back in the 70's. A *Guided Tour* of *Rutherford Hill* is included in *Tour No. 4*. However, you'll be *wine tasting only* on this visit.

If time left over, visit **Robert Sinskey Vineyards**, located near the corner of Silverado Trail and Yountville Crossroads. *Robert Sinskey* is also covered in *Tour No. 4*.

Facilities in Tour No. 2
Chateau Montelena, Cuvaison, Ehlers Estate, Trinchero Family Estates, Prager, Sutter Home

Chateau Montelena Winery

Cuvaison Winery

Ehlers Estate Winery

Trinchero Family Estates Winery (scheduled completion, Fall 2007)

Prager Port Works and Winery

Sutter Home Winery

Tour No. 2

Wineries in this itinerary will be equally dispersed along Highway 29 and the Silverado Trail

Chateau Montelena, Lunch, Cuvaison Winery, Ehlers Estate Winery, Trinchero Family Estates, Prager Port Works and Winery, Sutter Home Winery

<u>Chateau Montelena Winery</u> - *Guided Tour & Tasting* - 10:00 a.m. to 11:30 a.m.
Phone No. - 707-942-5105
Address - 1429 Tubbs Lane, Calistoga, California 94515
Web Site - www.chateaumontelena.com
Guided Tour & Tasting fee - $25.00 per person
Appointment required - Call in advance for reservations for the 10:00 a.m. *Guided Tour.*

The *Guided Tour* at *Chateau Montelena* lasts about an hour and one half. The winery is one of two facilities in the region that originally put the Napa Valley *"on the map."* It was selected as one of the best wines in a *"secret wine tasting"* held in France many years ago. You'll learn the whole story on your tour. Housed in an old medieval stone building located in stunning surroundings, the winery also has a beautiful lake on the premises. Visitors are welcome to stroll around the lake at their leisure. After *Chateau Montelena*, it's time for lunch. You'll have two options to choose from. Either have lunch in *Calistoga*, or pick up a picnic box lunch and take it to your next stop, *Cuvaison Winery*.

Lunch - Around 12:00 to 1:00 p.m.

Lunch Option No. 1
You can drive into Calistoga for lunch, just around the corner from *Chateau Montelena*. Check out the lunch options noted in *Tour No. 1*

Lunch Option No. 2
A few days prior to your visit, call ahead to the *Cal Mart Deli in Calistoga - 707-942-9686*. Order a gourmet box picnic lunch. They'll have it ready when you arrive. Then take your lunch to the picnic grounds at *Cuvaison Winery*, your next stop.

Cuvaison Winery - *Wine Tasting* - 1:00 p.m. to 1:30 p.m.
Phone No. - 707-942-6266
Address - 4550 Silverado Trail, Calistoga, California 94515
Web Site - www.cuvaison.com
Tasting fee - $10.00 Estate - $15.00 exclusives
No appointment required for wine tasting - 6 persons or less

   Cuvaison is a small picturesque winery along the *Silverado Trail*. Located in beautiful surroundings, the winery produces outstanding award winning wines. Well worth the stop! If you brought along a picnic lunch, enjoy it on the picnic grounds next to the winery.

Ehlers Estate Winery - *Wine Tasting* - 1:45 p.m. to 2:15 p.m.
Phone No. - 707-963-5972
Address - 3222 Ehlers Lane, St. Helena, California 94574
Web Site - www.ehlersestate.com
Tasting fee - $10.00 per person
No appointment required for wine tasting - 6 persons or less

   Ehlers Estate has always been one of my favorite small wineries. The facility is located down a peaceful country lane in a rustic old stone building next to an olive grove. The tasting room is comfortable and inviting. The winery produces outstanding Cabernets and Merlots, donating much of its profits to the American Heart Association for cardiovascular research. After *Ehlers Estate*, it's off to *Trinchero Family Estates*, a stone's throw away.

Trinchero Family Estates -*Wine Tasting* - 2:30 p.m. to 3:00 p.m.
Phone No. - 707-963-1160
Address - 3070 North St. Helena Highway, St. Helena, California 94574
Web Site - www.tfewines.com
No appointment required for wine tasting - 6 persons or less
Tasting Fee - Call ahead for tasting fees

Trinchero Family Estates Winery will be a stunning new facility. The site, formerly the *Folie a Deux Winery*, will serve as the new home for *Trinchero's* "Vine to Dine" programs featuring indoor and outdoor kitchens, wood-burning ovens, a reserve tasting room and cellar, plus an extensive culinary garden. The winery is scheduled for completion in the fall of 2007. Should it not be open at the time of your visit, substitute *Markham Vineyards*, just down the road. *Markham* is highlighted in *Tour No. 8*.

Prager Port Works & Winery - *Wine Tasting* - 3:15 p.m. to 3:45 p.m.
Phone No. - 707-963-7678
Address - 1281 Lewelling Lane, St. Helena, California 94574
Web Site - www.ahport@pragerport.com
Tasting fee - $10.00 per person
Appointment recommended for wine tasting. However, walk-ins usually accepted - 6 persons or less

Prager is a tucked away rustic gem located in an old barn building. It's one of very few wineries that produce both premium wines and outstanding ports. Wonderful aromas as you walk by old wine barrels to the tasting room. Appointments recommended since the tasting room is small. However, walk-in visitors are usually never turned away. But call ahead just in case.

Sutter Home Winery - *Wine Tasting* - 4:00 p.m. to 4:30 p.m.
Phone No. - 707-963-3104
Address - 277 St. Helena Highway, St. Helena, California 94574
Web Site - www.sutterhome.com
Tasting fee - Complimentary
No appointment required for wine tasting - 6 persons or less

Just about everyone's heard of *Sutter Home*, famous for its *White Zinfandel*. However, it also produces outstanding premium wines. The winery has a large tasting room plus an extensive gift shop. If visiting during the *Spring* or *Summer*, check out the wildflowers growing at the cottage adjacent to the winery.

If time left over after **Sutter Home**, choose another winery along the way. Check your tour map for facilities in the immediate area to see if they're still open.

Facilities in Tour No. 3
Raymond, Duckhorn, Rombauer,
Sterling, Ehlers Estate, St. Clement

Raymond Vineyards

Duckhorn Vineyards

Rombauer Vineyards

Sterling Vineyards

Ehlers Estate Winery

St. Clement Vineyards

Tour No. 3

South to North - Silverado Trail
Wineries located primarily along the Silverado Trail.

Raymond Vineyards, Lunch, Duckhorn Vineyards, Rombauer,
Sterling Vineyards, Ehlers Estate, St. Clement Vineyards

* Your *Guided Tour* won't begin until 1:00 p.m. at *Duckhorn Vineyards*. The tour is free, but you'll need a reservation. So call ahead and plan to arrive at *Duckhorn* no later than 12:45 p.m.

** *Lunch* - Plan for lunch around 11:30 a.m. Consider the lunch option listed below after visiting *Raymond Vineyards*.

<u>Raymond Vineyards</u> - *Wine Tasting* - 10:30 a.m. to 11:15 a.m.
Phone No. - 800-525-2659 or 707-963-3141
Address - 849 Zinfandel Lane, St. Helena, California 94574
Web Site - www.raymondvineyards.com
Tasting fee - $7.50 to $15.00 per person.
No appointment required for wine tasting - 6 persons or less

Raymond Vineyards is a small family owned winery producing premium wines. The Raymond's are fifth generation winemakers, rare in the Napa Valley. If you decided to visit *Raymond* prior to *Duckhorn*, make sure to leave no later than 11:15 a.m. This way, you'll have time for a casual lunch before arriving at *Duckhorn*.

Lunch - 11:30 a.m. to 12:30 p.m.

Stop into *Taylor's Refresher Drive In - 707-963-3486*, for lunch. You can eat your lunch there or take it with you. *Taylor's* is located at the south end of St. Helena on *Highway 29* across from *Merryvale Vineyards*. Check your tour map to find *Merryvale*. Consider calling in your order ahead. *Taylors* can get crowded, especially on weekends. After lunch, drive north a couple blocks to *Pope Street*. Go right on *Pope Street* and cut across to the *Silverado Trail*, then up to *Duckhorn Vineyards*, arriving at about 12:45 p.m. Check your tour map for directions. Don't drive through the town of St. Helena to get to Duckhorn. *Too much traffic!* Cut across to the Silverado Trail for a much easier drive up.

Duckhorn Vineyards - *Guided Tour & Tasting* - 1:00 p.m. to 2:00 p.m.
Phone No. - 866-367-9945 or 707-963-7108
Address - 1000 Lodi Lane, St. Helena, California 94574
Web Site - www.duckhorn.com
Tasting / Tour fee - Complimentary for tour. $10.00 to $20.00 per person for wine tasting depending upon program selected.
Appointment required - Call well in advance for reservations.
Duckhorn conducts one *complimentary tour* per day at 1:00 p.m.

Duckhorn Vineyards is located in a beautiful region along the *Silverado Trail*. The elegant tasting room is located in the *Vineyards Estate House*. One of the winery's specialties is Bordeaux style wines. *Duckhorn* was one of the first in the region to focus on Merlot as a premium wine. The winery produces four elegant Merlots and four distinctive Cabernets, plus other wines. Don't forget to take a stroll through the beautiful gardens while you're there. Well worth visiting this stunning facility.

Rombauer Vineyards - *Wine Tasting* - 2:15 p.m. to 2:45 p.m.

Rombauer was mentioned earlier in *Tour No. 1*. Since *Rombauer* is just up the road from *Duckhorn*, we decided to include it here. After *Rombauer*, it's up the Silverado Trail a short distance to *Sterling Vineyards*.

Sterling Vineyards - *Self Guided Tour & Wine Tasting* - 3:00 p.m. to 3:30 p.m.

Sterling was also mentioned in *Tour No. 1*. Refer to that tour for information. It can get a bit crowded on weekends, but worth the stop due to its geographical location.

Ehlers Estate Winery - *Wine Tasting* - 3:45 p.m. to 4:15 p.m.

Ehlers was also mentioned earlier in *Tour No. 2*. Refer to that tour for information. Next stop *St. Clement Vineyards* … just down the road.

St. Clement Vineyards - *Wine Tasting* - 4:30 p.m. to 5:00 p.m.
Phone No. - 800-331-8266
Address - 2867 St. Helena Highway North, St. Helena, California 94574
Web Site - www.stclement.com
Tasting fee - $10.00 per person
No appointment required for wine tasting - 6 persons or less

St. Clement is a small premium winery sitting atop a knoll just above *Highway 29*. The tasting room is located in a picturesque victorian mansion with commanding views of the vineyards. Outstanding wines plus magnificent surroundings. Well worth the stop!

Facilities in Tour No. 4
V. Sattui, Rutherford Hill, Robert Sinskey, Regusci, Clos Du Val, Signorello

V. Sattui Winery

Rutherford Hill Winery

Robert Sinskey Vineyards

Regusci Winery

Clos Du Val Winery

Signorello Vineyards

Tour No. 4

North to South - Silverado Trail
Most wineries located along the Silverado Trail.

V. Sattui Winery, Rutherford Hill, Lunch, Robert Sinskey,
Regusci Winery, Clos Du Val, Signorello Vineyards

* Your *Guided Tour* will be at *Rutherford Hill Winery* at 11:30 a.m.
Rutherford Hill Winery has three scheduled tours per day. Appointments
are not necessary. Visitors arrive about 10 to 15 minutes early to
register. However, call in advance to make sure a *Special Event* is not
being held.

** **Lunch** - I suggest having lunch after the tour at *Rutherford Hill
Winery*. The winery has a picnic grove with beautiful views of the
valley. A picnic lunch with wine would be a great alternative. We'll
look at this option plus others in a moment.

V. Sattui Winery - *Wine Tasting* - 10:15 a.m. to 11:00 a.m.
Phone No. - 707-963-7774
Address - 1111 White Lane, St. Helena, California 94574
Web Site - www.vsattui.com
Tasting fee - Complimentary - regular selections. Nominal fee -
reserve selections.
No appointment required for wine tasting - 6 persons or less

Located on *Highway 29*, the winery is a popular stop and can get
very crowded in season. However, by arriving early, you'll beat most of
the crowds. The winery offers complimentary tasting in their regular
tasting room, an extensive gourmet deli, and a wonderful gift shop. A
separate tasting room is also available for reserve wine tasting. There
is also a picnic grove on the property.

Suggestion for "lunch plans" after V. Sattui - Consider bringing along a styrofoam cooler packed with ice before your stop at *V. Sattui.* Once your finished wine tasting, buy your lunch in the deli, put it on ice, then head up to your next stop, *Rutherford Hill Winery.* Once you've completed your *Guided Tour* at *Rutherford Hill Winery,* enjoy your lunch at the less crowded picnic grounds on the premises. Magnificent views of the valley floor. Consider buying a bottle of their wine to enjoy with lunch. The picnic grounds are reserved for winery guests only, so it's always nice to return the favor with a little business.

Rutherford Hill Winery - *Guided Winery Tour and Tasting* - 11:30 a.m. to 12:30 p.m.
Phone No. - 707-963-7194
Address - 200 Rutherford Hill Road, Rutherford, California 94573
Web Site - *www.rutherfordhill.com*
Appointment not required. However, call ahead to make sure of availability.
Cost per person - About $15.00

Rutherford Hill was included in *Tour No. 1.* However, let's add some additional information here since you'll be taking a *Guided Tour* through the *Wine Caves.* The winery was one of the first to produce Merlot, one of Napa Valley's premier wines. It is also known for its extensive hillside cave system. The mile long caves maintain a year round temperature of 59 degree's and a constant humidity of 90%, the perfect atmosphere for aging wine. The *Guided Tour* includes a walk through the *Wine Caves* and wine tasting in the cellar.

Lunch - 12:30 p.m. to 1:15 p.m.

If you've brought along your picnic lunch, enjoy it on the picnic grounds next to the winery. Otherwise, a good bet for eating inside is the *Rutherford Grill - 707-963-1792,* located about 10 minutes away in the town of *Rutherford.* It's the main restaurant in town at the intersection of *Highway 29* and *Rutherford Crossroad.* Reservations are not taken. Just show up on a first come first served basis. Another fantastic upscale restaurant is *Auberge du Soleil,* just below *Rutherford Hill Winery.* It was mentioned in *Part 10. 707-963-1211.* Advance reservations always required. After lunch, it's back on the road for more wine tasting.

Robert Sinskey Vineyards - *Wine Tasting* - 1:30 p.m. to 2:00 p.m.
Phone No. - 800-869-2030 or 707-944-9090
Address - 6320 Silverado Trail, Napa, California 94558
Web Site - www.robertsinskey.com
Tasting fee - $15.00 regular selections - $20.00 reserves
No appointment required for wine tasting - 6 persons or less

   Robert Sinskey Vineyards is located on the *Silverado Trail* in the famous *Stags Leap Appellation*. The winery has beautiful views of the lower valley floor. In addition, it has its own gourmet kitchen and can provide *Special Wine and Food Events* for groups. Please call for details. After *Robert Sinskey*, it's on to our next stop, *Regusci Winery*.

Regusci Winery - *Wine Tasting* - 2:15 p.m. to 2:45 p.m.
Phone No. - 707-254-0403
Address - 5584 Silverado Trail, Napa, California 94558
Web site - www.regusciwinery.com
Tasting fee - $10.00 per person
Appointments recommended. However, walk-ins usually accepted - 6 persons or less

   A long time favorite of mine, *Regusci* is just down the road from *Robert Sinskey Vineyards*. The term *Ghost Winery* is usually given to the few remaining winery buildings that were in existence between 1860 and 1900. The building at *Regusci* is one of these well preserved *Ghost Wineries*. The production of grapes on the property was re-established by the *Regusci* family in 1996. The vineyards are famous for producing premier grapes also used by several other wineries in the region. Although the family could produce larger vintages, they instead choose to produce limited quantities of outstanding Merlots, Cabernets, and Zinfandels. The winery sits well off the *Silverado Trail* at the base of the mountains. It has a rustic farm like atmosphere with stunning views of the valley looking west. Many winery tour maps indicate *Regusci* requires an appointment for wine tasting. However, I've never been turned away at the door. Just show up and you'll be welcomed at this friendly down home winery. But if in on a weekend, call ahead just in case.

Clos Du Val Winery - *Wine Tasting* - 3:00 p.m. to 3:30 p.m.
Phone No. - 707-261-5200
Address - 5330 Silverado Trail, Napa, California 94558
Web Site - www.closduval.com
No appointment required for wine tasting only - 6 persons or less
Tasting fee - $10.00 per person
Reserve Tasting Fee - Weekends only - $20.00 per person

Located in the famous *Stags Leap Appellation, Clos Du Val* has been producing award winning wines since 1972. Another great stop in an area with spectacular scenery.

Signorello Vineyards - *Wine Tasting* - 3:45 p.m. to 4:15 p.m.
Phone No. - 707-255-5990
Address - 4500 Silverado Trail, Napa, California 94558
Web Site - www.signorellovineyards.com
Appointment required for wine tasting. However, walk-ins usually accepted - 6 persons or less
Tasting fee - $10.00 per person

Signorello is located high atop a knoll overlooking the lower Napa Valley. This small family owned facility offers outstanding wines, a beautiful environment, and a commanding view of the valley floor. This is one of the few wineries in the area where you can look across the entire lower valley basin. Most winery tour maps indicate an appointment is required; however, I've never been turned away by merely showing up.

If time left over, visit **Darioush** just down the road. **Darioush** closes at 5:00 p.m. Check your tour map for details on this facility.

Facilities in Tour No. 5
Monticello, Del Dotto Caves,
Reynolds Family, Regusci, Goosecross, Cliff Lede

Monticello Vineyards

Del Dotto Caves Winery

Reynolds Family Winery

Regusci Winery

Harvest Time at Goosecross

Cliff Lede Vineyards

Tour No. 5

Lower Napa Valley Region - Silverado Trail

*Monticello Vineyards, Del Dotto Caves Winery, Lunch,
Reynolds Family Winery, Regusci Winery, Goosecross*

* On this tour, you'll visit one winery in the morning before your *Guided Tour* at *Del Dotto Caves Winery*.

Monticello Vineyards - *Wine Tasting* - 10:00 a.m. to 10:30 a.m.
Phone No. - 707-253-2802
Address - 4242 Big Ranch Road, Napa, California 94558
Web Site - www.monticellovineyards.com
No appointment required for wine tasting - 6 persons or less
Tasting fee - $10.00 per person

Located on the outskirts of Napa, *Monticello Vineyards* is a replica of Thomas Jefferson's home bearing the same name. The Corley family has been producing outstanding premium wines here for some time. A great stop in the lower valley for premium wine tasting plus historic nostalgia. After *Monticello*, your off for your *Guided Tour* at *Del Dotto Caves Winery*. Make sure to arrive at *Del Dotto* no later than 10:45 a.m. to register.

Del Dotto Caves Winery - *Guided Tour - Cave Tour and Wine Tasting* -
11:00 a.m. to 12:30 p.m.
Appointment required - Call well in advance for reservation
Phone No. - 707-256-3332
Address - 1055 Atlas Peak Road, Napa, California 94559
Web Site - www.deldottovineyards.com
Tour and Tasting fee - $40.00 per person. Tasting only at wine bar - $10.00 - $20.00 per person

Del Dotto Caves Winery is a fascinating place to visit. Although the fee for the *Guided Tour* at this premier facility may stretch your budget, it's well worth it. The *Wine Cave* is one of only about six left in the region that were originally dug by hand around the turn of the century. Most other caves in the area have been excavated by large cave digging machines. At *Del Dotto*, you'll enjoy an extensive tour of the cave, do some tasting from actual wine barrels, then go back to the tasting room for additional wine tasting. Located in a rustic old stone building, the facility also has an extensive international wine collection. Well worth the price if you can afford it!

Lunch - 12:45 p.m. to 1:45 p.m. - Four (4) lunch options to choose from:

Option No. 1 - *Monticello Deli* - *Deli / Picnic Style* -707-255-3953 - *1810 Monticello Road*. The *Monticello Deli* is just around the corner from *Del Dotto Caves Winery*. Deli sandwiches, drinks, plus other items.

Option No. 2 - *The Grill at Silverado Resort* -707-257-0200. A more upscale restaurant, *The Grill* offers outstanding dining in a resort style atmosphere. Reservations suggested, especially on weekends.

Option No. 3 - *Soda Canyon Store* - *Deli / Picnic Style* - 707-252-0285. The *Soda Canyon Store* is located not far north at the corner of *Silverado Trail* and *Soda Canyon Road*. It offers deli style sandwiches, drinks and other items. Several picnic tables are located on the property.

Option No. 4 - *Yountville*
There are several restaurants to choose from in town. Go to *www. napavalley.com*, click on *Yountville*, then click on *dining*. You can also check out the restaurants listed for *Yountville* in *Part 10*.

Reynolds Family Winery - *Wine Tasting* - 2:00 p.m. to 2:30 p.m.
Phone No. - 707-258-2558
Address - 3266 Silverado Trail, Napa, California 94558
Web Site - www.reynoldsfamiliywinery.com
Appointment required for wine tasting
Tasting fee - $10.00 per person

Reynolds Family Winery is a small facility specializing in limited production premier Cabernet Sauvignon. The winery sits off the *Silverado Trail* at the foot of the *Stags Leap District* in the proposed *Silverado Bench Appellation*. This area is known for producing rich and complex wines. Located in a truly beautiful setting, this is a perfect stop for wine tasting in comfortable surroundings.

Regusci Winery - *Wine Tasting* - 3:00 p.m. to 3:30 p.m.

Always one of my favorite places to visit, this is the second time I've mentioned *Regusci*. Since it's along our route, we'll include it here. See *Tour No. 4* for a description. After *Regusci*, it's off to our next stop, *Goosecross Winery*. Take note, *Goosecross* closes to visitors at 4:00 p.m.

Goosecross Winery - *Wine Tasting* - 3:45 p.m. to 4:15 p.m.
Phone No. - 800-276-9210 or 707- 944-1986
Address - 1119 State Lane, Yountville, California 94599
Web Site - www.goosecross.com
Appointment required. However, walk-ins usually accepted. - 6 persons or less
Tasting fee - $5.00 per person

Goosecross is a small family owned facility located in the lower Napa Valley. The winery sits at the end of a peaceful lane with open views of the *Stags Leap District* to the east, and the *Mayacamus Mountains* to the west. The tasting room is small, but very inviting as you walk past large wine barrels stacked one upon another. The wine aromas in the air and the friendly staff make this a great stop for some premium wine tasting. Appointments are usually requested. However, I've never been turned away showing up unannounced. Because the tasting room can get a bit crowded, it might be best to call ahead before you arrive to check out the situation.

If time left over after *Goosecross*, visit **Cliff Lede Vineyards** just down the road. Check your map for the location. **Cliff Lede** is part of *Tour No. 6*. Please refer to that tour for details.

Facilities in Tour No. 6
Hess Collection, Laird Family Estate, Domaine Chandon,
Diamond Oaks, Cliff Lede, Miner Family

Hess Collection Winery

Laird Family Estate Winery

Domaine Chandon Winery

Diamond Oaks Winery

Cliff Lede Vineyards

Miner Family Vineyards

Tour No. 6

For Contemporary Art Lovers - Lower Napa Valley Region
Hess Collection, Laird Family Estate, Lunch, Domaine Chandon,
Diamond Oaks Winery, Cliff Lede Vineyards, Miner Family Vineyards

Hess Collection Winery - *Self Guided Tour & Wine Tasting* - 10:00 a.m. to 11:00 a.m.
Phone No. - 707-255-1144
Address - 4411 Redwood Road, Napa, California 94558
Web Site - www.hesscollection.com - Check Web Site for DIRECTIONS MAP
No appointment needed for "Self Guided" tour & wine tasting - 6 persons or less
Tasting Fee - $10.00 Regular - $16.00 Library Cabs

   Hess Collection Winery is a 15 minute ride west from *Highway 29*. Follow *Redwood Road* to the signs leading up to the winery. Check your tour map for directions. In addition, go to their web site and check out the *Directions Map*. Located in a beautiful mountain setting, the winery has three floors of contemporary art on continuous display. After your *Self Guided Tour*, you can enjoy wine tasting in a comfortable tasting room or visit the extensive gift shop. This facility has it all and is a great way to begin your day.

Laird Family Estate Winery - *Wine Tasting* - 11:15 a.m. to 11:45 a.m.
Phone No. - 877-297-4902 or 707-257-0360
Address - 5055 Solano Avenue, Napa, California 94558
Web Site - www.lairdfamilyestate.com
Appointment required - But drop-ins OK - 6 persons or less
Tasting fee - $10.00 per person

Laird Family Estate is located off *Highway 29* on Solano Avenue, just north of the Oak Knoll Avenue intersection. Look for the blue pyramid shaped roof. The winery specializes in premium, single vineyard varieties. Another great stop before lunch.

Lunch - Yountville - 12:00 to 1:00 p.m.

Just up the road from *Laird* is the town of *Yountville*. You've got several options here. The *Lakeside Grill* at the *Vintners Golf Course - 707-944-2426* is on the way. It offers lunch with fantastic views across the golf course to the western hills. The *Napa Valley Grill - 707-944-8686*, is another local favorite. Reservations always suggested. *Pacific Blues Cafe - 707-944-4455*, is a laid back cafe outside the *Vintage 1870* shopping complex. Then there's *Compadres Restaurant* for great Mexican cuisine - *707-944-2406*. One of the finest restaurants in the Napa Valley is located at *Domaine Chandon Winery - 707-944-2280*, which just happens to be our next stop. Reservations always suggested. There is a casual dress code requirement. Check it out on their web site at *www.chandon.com*. At the time of publication, the restaurant at *Domaine Chandon* was closed Tuesdays and Wednesdays.

Many other fine restaurants are located in the area. Research them on line at *www.napavalley.com*. Click on *Yountville*, then *dining*.

Domaine Chandon Winery - *Wine Tasting* - 1:15 p.m. to 1:45 p.m.
Phone No. - 707-944-2280
Address - 1 California Drive, Yountville, California 94559
Web Site - www.chandon.com
No appointment required for wine tasting - 6 persons or less
Tasting fee - $10.00 to $30.00 per person depending on selections.

Domaine Chandon is one of the premier *Sparkling Wine* producers in the world. This beautiful facility has plenty of parking, gorgeous grounds, an extensive gift shop, and superb *Sparkling Wine*. A perfect stop after lunch.

Diamond Oaks Winery - *Wine Tasting* - 2:00 p.m. to 2:30 p.m.
Phone No. - 707-948-3000
Address - 1595 Oakville Grade, Oakville, California 94562
Web Site - www.diamond-oaks.com
No appointment required for wine tasting - 6 persons or less
Tasting fee - $7.00 per person

   Diamond Oaks is just a short distance up the road from *Domaine Chandon*. The unique thing about *Diamond Oaks* is not only its outstanding wines, but the location. Head up *Highway 29* to the *Oakville Grade Road* on the left. Go up *Oakville Grade* to the winery on the left. The facility has a fantastic view of the valley. A great stop for wine tasting and relaxation. *Diamond Oaks* also has a picnic grove with breathtaking views. However, picnic tables must be reserved in advance. After your visit, head back down the *Oakville Grade*, then east across *Oakville Crossroad* to the *Silverado Trail*. Go south on the *Silverado Trail* a short distance to the *Yountville Crossroad*, where you'll visit our next gem, *Cliff Lede Vineyards*.

Cliff Lede Vineyards - *Wine Tasting* - 2:45 p.m. to 3:15 p.m.
Phone No. - 800-428-2259 or 707-944-8642
Address - 1473 Yountville Crossroad, Yountville, California 94599
Web site - www.cliffledevineyards.com
No appointment required for wine tasting - 6 persons or less
Tasting fee -$10.00 per person

   Cliff Lede Vineyards was founded in 2002, but the facility has a history dating back many years. Located in the *Stags Leap District*, the winery is easy to find along the *Yountville Crossroad*. This beautiful facility offers an outstanding atmosphere with magnificent views from the patio. After *Cliff Lede*, it's back up the *Silverado Trail* a short distance to our next stop, *Miner Family Vineyards*.

Miner Family Vineyards - *Wine Tasting* - 3:30 p.m. to 4:00 p.m.
Phone No. - 800-366-9463
Address - 7850 Silverado Trail, Oakville, California 94562
Web Site - www.minerwines.com
No appointment required for wine tasting - 6 persons or less
Tasting fee - $10.00 per person

Miner Family Vineyards is located on the *Silverado Trail* a short distance up from *Cliff Lede Vineyards.* The multi story facility offers guests award winning wines plus a commanding view of the valley from the terrace.

If time left over, visit **Steltzner Vineyards,** not far down the *Silverado Trail.*

Facilities in Tour No. 7
Hess Collection, Andretti, Monticello, Trefethen,
Domaine Chandon, Robert Mondavi

Hess Collection Winery

Andretti Winery

Monticello Vineyards

Trefethen Vineyards

Domaine Chandon Winery

Robert Mondavi Winery

Tour No. 7

Again, for Contemporary Art Lovers - Lower Region

Hess Collection, Lunch, Andretti Winery, Monticello, Trefethen Vineyards, Domaine Chandon, Robert Mondavi

* We're going to include **Hess Collection Winery** again in this tour ... but start out a little later in the morning for you *"late risers"* ... plus include some additional lower Napa Valley region wineries to consider.

<u>Hess Collection Winery</u> - *Self Guided Tour & Wine Tasting* - 10:30 a.m. to 11:30 a.m.
Phone No. - 707-255-1144
Address - 4411 Redwood Road, Napa, California, 94558
Web Site - www.hesscollection.com - Check Web Site for *Directions Map*
No appointment needed for "Self Guided" tour & wine tasting - 6 persons or less
Tasting Fee - $10.00 Regular - $16.00 Library Cabs

Hess Collection Winery was also included in the previous tour, *Tour No. 6*. Please refer to that tour for details on this facility. We've included it again here because of the unique things it has to offer, plus added additional lower region wineries to the tour.

Lunch - 12:00 to 1:00 p.m. - Consider the same lunch options recommended in *Tour No. 6*

<u>Andretti Winery</u> - *Wine Tasting* - 1:15 p.m. to 1:45 p.m.
Phone No. - 888-460-8463 or 707-255-3524
Address - 4162 Big Ranch Road, Napa, California 94558

Web Site - www.andrettiwinery.com
No appointment required for wine tasting - 6 persons or less
Tasting fee - $8.00 - regular selections. $12.00 - reserves

Andretti Winery is located on *Big Ranch Road*. The winery has an interesting background. It was established in 1996 by Mario Andretti, widely regarded as one of the greatest race car drivers of all time. His passion and love of wine influenced him to open the winery, concentrating on the production of limited edition premium wines. The building and tasting room have a wonderful charm, portraying an integral part of the Tuscan style Andretti Villa.

Monticello Vineyards - *Wine Tasting* - 2:00 p.m. to 2:30 p.m.

A stones throw from *Andretti Winery*, we've already mentioned *Monticello* in *Tour No. 5*. Refer to that tour for a description of *Monticello*. The winery is included here due to its close proximity.

Trefethen Vineyards - *Wine Tasting* - 2:45 p.m. to 3:15 p.m.
Phone No. - 707-255-7700
Address - 1160 Oak Knoll Road, Napa, California 94558
Web Site - www.trefethen.com
No appointment required for wine tasting - 6 persons or less
Tasting fee - $10.00 per person / estate wines - $20.00 per person / reserve wines
Visitors also receive a complimentary taste of Estate Dry Riesling

Trefethen is the only surviving example of what was once the most common architecture in the Napa Valley, a three story wooden gravity flow system. The facility was designed and built in 1886 and was originally known as *Eshcol*. The building was in severe disrepair for almost 30 years until the present owners purchased it in 1968, restoring it to its former glory. Located in a beautiful setting, the interesting architecture and outstanding wines make it a must stop on this tour. After *Trefethen*, it's off to our next stop, *Domaine Chandon*.

<u>Domaine Chandon</u> - *Sparkling Wine Tasting* - 3:30 p.m. to 4:00 p.m.
Closed Mondays and Tuesdays during winter

See *Tour No. 6* for a description of the winery. *Domaine Chandon* is included due to its geographical location.

<u>Robert Mondavi Winery</u> - *Wine Tasting* - 4:15 p.m. to 4:45 p.m.
Phone No. - 1-888-766-6328
Address - Highway 29, Oakville, California 94562
Web Site - www.robertmondavi.com
No appointment required for standard wine tasting - 6 persons or less
Tasting Fee - $5.00 to $20.00 on up, depending upon wines tasted.

Robert Mondavi Winery is located in the town of *Oakville* just north of *Yountville*. This famous facility is housed in a beautiful Spanish style building with the *Mayacaymus Mountains* serving as a stunning backdrop to the west. The winery is a popular stop along *Highway 29,* offering outstanding wines and educational programs.

Facilities in Tour No. 8
*Burgess Cellars, Rombauer, Ehlers Estate,
St. Clement, Markham, "CIA"*

Burgess Cellars

Rombauer Vineyards

Ehlers Estate Winery

St. Clement Vineyards

Markham Vineyards

The CIA — Culinary Institute of America

Tour No. 8

A Napa Valley "Cooking Experience"
Includes visiting the "CIA" - Culinary Institute of America

Burgess Cellars, Rombauer, Ehlers Estate, Lunch,
St. Clement, Markham, "CIA"

We're going to build this tour around the *Culinary Institute of America's* live cooking demonstrations. The *"CIA"* offers classes at different times during the week, but we'll choose the 3:30 p.m. weekend class here. The *"CIA"* is one of the foremost *Culinary Arts Colleges* in the country. Many of the worlds greatest chefs have studied here. Located north of *St. Helena* in a massive old stone building that once housed the famous *Christian Brothers Winery*, the facility is also home to the *Spectator Restaurant at Greystone*, one of the premier restaurants in the region. At the time of publication, the *"CIA"* continued to offer *Live Cooking Demonstrations* to the general public for a nominal fee. The demonstrations are held in an open theater with excellent viewing from all seats. Audiovisual aids are also used, including overhead screens that enhance the viewing pleasure. Classes last about an hour and one half. Participants can then taste the prepared food at the end. Over the years, I've attended many of these classes. There's something special about actually observing a skilled chef prepare gourmet food in person. You can do this at the *"CIA"* cooking demonstrations. Menu's generally change for each demonstration and can be obtained in advance by either calling the *"CIA"* or going to their web site. This is a great alternative if you enjoy gourmet cooking or are merely interested in a different and unique experience. *www.ciachef.edu/california/demonstrations.asp*

Burgess Cellars - *Wine Tasting* - 10:00 a.m. to 10:30 a.m.
Phone No. - 800-752-9463 or 707-963-4766
Address - 1108 Deer Park Road, St. Helena, California 94574
Web Site - www.burgesscellars.com
Appointment required during the week. Appointment not required on weekends, but advise calling ahead.
Tasting fee - Complimentary tasting

    Burgess Cellars is located in a rustic stone and redwood building on a mountainside. The winery had its original beginnings in the 1880's. Well worth the stop at this unique small family winery. Outstanding world class wines and what has been referred to as the *"Best View of the Napa Valley."*

Rombauer Vineyards - *Wine Tasting* - 10:45 a.m. to 11:15 a.m.

    *Rombaue*r was already mentioned several times. Refer to *Tour No. 1* for information on this winery.

Ehlers Estate Winery - *Wine Tasting* - 11:30 a.m. to 12:00

    Ehlers Estate was also covered earlier in *Tour No. 2*. Refer to that tour for details.

Lunch - 12:00 to 1:00 p.m. - Two (2) Lunch Options:

Option No. 1 - *Taylor's Refresher* - Mentioned in *Tour No. 3*. Check out the details there.

Option No. 2 - *Wine Spectator Greystone Restaurant at the CIA* - 707-967-1010
Web Site - *www.ciachef.edu/restaurants/wsgr/*

    You'll be visiting the *"CIA"* later in the day for your cooking demonstration. Located at the *"CIA,"* the *Spectator Restaurant* is well worth visiting. You can dine inside or on the terrace with spectacular views across the valley. A unique dining experience offering California Wine Country cuisine. Reservations always recommended.

St. Clement Vineyards - *Wine Tasting* - 1:30 p.m. to 2:00 p.m.

St. Clement is another beautiful gem along the way. Refer to *Tour No. 3* for a description of this facility.

Markham Vineyards - *Wine Tasting* - 2:15 p.m. to 2:45 p.m.

Phone No. - 707-963-5292
Address - 2812 St. Helena Highway North, St. Helena, California 94574
Web Site - www.markhamvineyards.com
No appointment required for wine tasting - 6 persons or less
Tasting fee - regular - $5.00 - *Hard To Find Wines* - $8.00 - *Reserves* - $15.00

Markham is only a stone's throw away from your next stop, the *"CIA."* Drop into *Markham* and taste some outstanding award winning wines. After *Markham*, you may have some time left over. If so, drop into the *"CIA"* early and visit the *Campus Store Culinary Gift Shop.* You won't be disappointed!

The CIA - Cooking Demonstration Class - 3:30 p.m. to 5:00 p.m.

Phone No. - 707-967-2320
Address - 2555 Main Street, St. Helena, California, 94574
Web site - www.ciachef.edu/california/demonstrations.asp
Live Cooking Demonstrations
Appointment required in advance
Mon. & Fri. - 1:30 p.m. and 3:30 p.m.
Week ends - 10:30 a.m., 1:30 p.m., and 3:30 p.m.
Cost per person - $15.00

Facilities in Tour No. 9
Swanson, Beaulieu,
Caymus, Conn Creek, ZD, Miner Family

Swanson Vineyards

Beaulieu Vineyards

Caymus Vineyards

Conn Creek Winery

ZD Wines

Miner Family Vineyards

Tour No. 9

Exclusive "Private Tasting" Itinerary

Swanson Vineyards, Lunch, Beaulieu Vineyard,
Caymus, Conn Creek Winery, ZD, Miner Family

Many wineries in the region offer *Exclusive Private Events* that can be scheduled by simply calling in advance. They include private tastings, luncheons, dinners, and other affairs. Fees for such events can be nominal to expensive, depending upon the event, number of persons involved, and the food or wines served. The following tour includes a unique *Private Wine Tasting* experience in spectacular surroundings. However, it is by no means the only alternative available. It just happens to be one of many I've conducted over the years. For example, let's say you've got a *Special Winery* in mind you've always wanted to visit, but hoped a more exclusive *Private Event* was available for you and your guest(s). Chances are your winery offers such a program. Simply call and ask if they can arrange a *Private Tasting*. You might be surprised to find they can. But remember, the fee for such events is usually much higher than the normal fee charged for regular wine tasting.

Swanson Vineyards - *Private Wine Tasting* - * 10:00 a.m. to 12:00
Phone No. - 707-967-3500
Address - 1271 Manley Lane, Rutherford, California 94573
Web Site - www.swansonvineyards.com
Appointment always required
Cost per person - Approximately $25.00 to $55.00 depending upon program selected.

* The time for this tasting could vary depending upon prior scheduling and the number of persons involved. I've attended many private tastings at *Swanson*. If you call well ahead, an appointment can usually

be arranged in the morning. However, the operative words here are *call well ahead*. So let's assume you've been able to schedule the 10:00 a.m. *Private Tasting* at *Swanson*. Here's how it works.

The *Private Wine Tasting* lasts about 2 hours and is limited to approximately 8 guests. If it's just two of you, expect to be paired at the table with 6 other people. Don't worry, you'll all get along fine. Chances are it's a first time experience for everyone anyway. There are usually two programs offered, *Standard Releases* or more exclusive *Limited Edition Reserve Wines*. At the time of publication, *Swanson* was still offering these two programs. Upon arriving, your greeted by a hostess and escorted into a spectacular tasting room. In the middle of the room is an elegant table adorned with fine linen's and beautiful wine glasses. Your host begins by explaining the history of the winery. After this, you'll taste world class wines paired with special delicacies. Such an event should be experienced at least once during a visit to the Napa Valley. After *Swanson*, it's off to the *Rutherford Grill* for lunch, just up the road.

Lunch - 12:00 to 1:00 p.m.

Rutherford Grill - *707-963-1792 - 1180 Rutherford Road, Rutherford, California 94573*

Mentioned in *Tour No. 4*, the *Rutherford Grill* is a local favorite. California Wine Country cuisine in a wonderful environment. Reservations not taken, so be ready for a short wait … especially on weekends.

Beaulieu Vineyard - *Wine Tasting* - 1:15 p.m. to 1:45 p.m.
Phone No. - 800-264-6918 or 707-967-5200
Address - 1960 St. Helena Highway, Rutherford, California 94573
Web Site - www.bvwines.com
No appointment required for wine tasting - 6 persons or less
Tasting fee - $10.00 main selections - $25.00 reserve wines

Beaulieu Vineyard is located next to the *Rutherford Grill*, a convenient stop for wine tasting. You can walk to the tasting room from the restaurant. Known as "BV" in the valley, the winery has been producing award winning wines for years. After *BV*, take a short drive down *Rutherford Crossroad* to your next stop, *Caymus Vineyards*. *Caymus* requires an appointment, so call well in advance.

Caymus Vineyards - *Wine Tasting* - 2:00 p.m. to 2:30 p.m.
Phone No. - 707-963-4204
Address - 8700 Conn Creek Road, Rutherford, California 94573
Web Site - www.caymus.com
Appointment required - Call in advance, especially for weekend visits.
Tasting fee - Complimentary wine tasting

Caymus Vineyards is a small family owned winery founded in 1972. The winery obtains most of its grapes from vineyards in the *Rutherford District* and specializes in only one wine, Cabernet Sauvignon. Located in beautiful surroundings, this award winning facility is a perfect stop along the way.

Conn Creek Winery - *Wine Tasting* - 2:45 p.m. to 3:15 p.m.
Phone No. - 707-963-9100
Address - 8711 Silverado Trail, St. Helena, California 94574
Web Site - www.conncreekwinery.com
No appointment required for wine tasting - 6 persons or less
Tasting fee - $10.00 per person

Conn Creek Winery was established in 1973. Since then, it has been producing some of California's finest limited edition Cabernet Sauvignon and other Bordeaux style wines. The Mediterranean style building and its picturesque garden make it a great stop. Wine theme gifts are also available. After *Conn Creek*, it's just a short drive down the *Silverado Trail* to your next stop, *ZD Wines*.

ZD Wines - *Wine Tasting* - 3:30 p.m. to 4:00 p.m.
Phone No. - 800-487-7757 or 707-963-5188
Address - 8383 Silverado Trail, Napa, California 94558
Web Site - www.zdwines.com
No appointment required for wine tasting - 6 persons or less
Tasting fee - $10.00 to $15.00 per person

ZD Wines is another beautiful small winery along the *Silverado Trail*. The facility produces limited award winning premium wines and has a wonderful view looking west across the valley floor.

If time left over, stop in at **Miner Family Vineyards**, mentioned earlier in *Tour No. 6.*

Facilities in Tour No. 10
Option 1— Monday–Friday
Chappellet, Rustridge, Rutherford Hill

Chappellet Vineyards

Rustridge Winery

Rutherford Hill Winery

Facilities in Tour No. 10

Option 2 — Saturday only
Kuleto Estate, Nichelini, Rustridge

Kuleto Estate Winery

Nichelini Winery

Rustridge Winery

Tour No. 10

"Off the Beaten Path" Winery Tour

Option No. 1 - Monday through Friday only
Chappellet Vineyards, Lunch, Rustridge, Rutherford Hill

Option No. 2 - Saturday only
Kuleto Estate, Lunch, Nichelini, Rustridge

If you feel like really exploring the countryside, this is the tour for you. There are many wonderful small wineries in rural parts of the Napa Valley. They're located in beautiful surroundings within easy driving distance from most points. However, visitors don't often get out to these gems for two reasons. First, the more *"well known"* wineries are located along the two major routes on the main valley floor; *Highway 29* and the *Silverado Trail*. These are a bit more convenient to drive to. Second, most visitors are unaware of the facilities in the outer regions. Yet, these *diamonds in the rough* offer just what one might be looking for; small friendly atmospheres, less crowds, outstanding wines, and spectacular scenery. If your looking for a unique experience, consider this tour. Depending upon the day(s) you'll be visiting, you'll have two options to choose from. So pick the tour that best fits with your schedule. You won't be able to visit as many wineries in a day, but I guarantee you'll be thoroughly satisfied with the tours listed here.

These rural facilities welcome visitors, but require an appointment for either a tour or tasting. Make sure to have your *WINERY TOUR MAP* in possession for directions. The wineries highlighted are on most maps. However, if unsure, confirm directions when calling for your appointment. Directions are also given on the winery web sites. So check out this source as well.

There are no restaurants in the area, so you'll need to consider a *picnic lunch*. Either the night before or during the early morning of

115

your tour, obtain a styrofoam cooler, pack it with ice, and buy some lunch fixings at a local supermarket or deli. Then pack it up for your *Off the Beaten Path Tour*. Most of the wineries you'll be visiting have picnic tables. Talk about a fun way to spend a day! ... *Mind if I join you?*

Anyway, the wineries in this tour are located primarily in the same geographical region. Depending upon the day of the week you choose, you'll begin your tour at either *Chappellet Vineyards* or *Kuleto Estates.*

I've always felt the best days to visit *Chappellet* were Monday through Friday. If you can plan your tour for any of these days, choose *Option No. 1*, placing *Chappellet* on the list for your first stop. *Chappellet* has a regularly scheduled *Tour and Tasting* twice daily, the first at 10:30 a.m. You'll need an appointment in advance. On the other hand, if visiting on a weekend, you must choose *Option No. 2* for a *Saturday*, making *Kuleto Estate* your first stop.

Depending upon the day you choose, your schedule will look like this. If in on a Monday through Friday, your itinerary will be *Option No. 1 - Chappellet, Lunch, Rustridge, and Rutherford Hill* ... with time left over for possibly one more.

If in on a weekend, you must choose *Option No. 2* and schedule your tour for *Saturday*, Your itinerary will be *Kuleto Estate, Lunch, Nichelini, Rustridge.*

OK ... ready for this exciting trek? If so ... it's *Off the Beaten Path we go!*

"Off the Beaten Path" Tour
Option No. 1 - Monday through Friday

Chappellet Vineyards - *Guided Tour and Wine Tasting* - 10:30 a.m. to 12:00
Phone No. - 707-963-7136 or 800-4 WINERY
Address - 1581 Sage Canyon Road, St. Helena, California, 94574
Web Site - www.chappellet.com
Appointment required in advance
Days of week - Open Monday through Saturday
Tour and tasting fee - $15.00 per person

Chappellet sits about 1200 feet above the valley floor with spectacular vistas traveling up to the winery. The atmosphere is serene and

very peaceful. This family owned wine⌐
and emphasizes preserving the land th⌐
techniques. *Chappellet* produces outstandi⌐

Directions to Chappellet - Have your tour ma⌐
128 from the *Silverado Trail* driving toward L⌐
the lake to the boat ramp and parking lot on⌐
parking lot are three driveways. Turn right at t⌐
see the mail box labeled *Pritchard Hill*. Follow ⌐way up the hill
about 1.5 miles to the winery. Breathtaking views looking back down
the valley to *Lake Hennessey*. If in doubt about directions, check the
winery web site.

Lunch - 12:00 to 1:00 p.m.

You'll finish around noon at *Chappellet*. You can then enjoy your picnic
lunch back down the road anywhere near *Lake Hennessey*, or possibly
right at the winery.

<u>Rustridge Winery</u> - *Wine Tasting* - 1:30 p.m. to 2:30 p.m.
Phone - 800-788-0263 or 707-965-9353
Address - 2910 Lower Chiles Valley Road, St. Helena, California 94574
Web Site - www.rustridge.com
Appointment required - Call in advance
Tasting fee - $10.00 per person

    Rustridge is located in a ranch like setting in Chiles Valley, a region
known to produce outstanding Cabernet Sauvignon and Zinfandel
wines. A Bed and Breakfast Inn is also located on the property. Although
rural, the winery takes you away from the hustle and clatter of the
crowds. Just beyond peaceful Lake Hennessey, the ranch is located on
450 acres where you'll experience sweeping views of vineyards, pastures,
playful foals and ancient oak trees. Since the 1950's, the ranch has been
a breeding and training facility for thoroughbred race horses. The Bed
& Breakfast Inn offers feather beds, private baths, decks, and delicious
breakfasts. If choosing the " Off the Beaten Path "tour... Option No. 1,
make sure to go to the Rustridge web site for a map and directions.

Winery - *Wine tasting* - 3:00 p.m. to 3:45 p.m.

d Hill was covered in *Tour No. 4.* Please refer to that tour for
ls.

If time left over, choose another winery within the same geographical area. Make sure it's open to the public. Check your tour map for such facilities.

"Off the Beaten Path" Tour
Option No. 2 - Saturday only

Kuleto Estate Winery - *Guided Tour and Wine Tasting* - 10:30 a.m. to 12:00
Phone No. - 707-963-9750
Address - 2470 Sage Canyon Road, St. Helena, California 94574
Web Site - www.kuleto.com
Appointment required - Call in advance
Tour / Tasting fee - $25.00 per person

Kuleto Estate was established in 1992 by culinary entrepreneur Pat Kuleto. The winery is located in a beautiful area overlooking *Lake Hennessey, Pritchard Hill,* and the communities of *Rutherford* and *St. Helena.* A truly spectacular place to visit with unparalleled scenic beauty. One of the Napa Valley's best kept secrets. Use your map for directions or go to the winery web site for a *Directions Map.*

Lunch - 12:30 p.m. to 1:30 p.m. You can enjoy your picnic lunch on the grounds at *Kuleto.*

Nichelini Winery - *Wine Tasting* - 1:45 p.m. to 2:15 p.m.
Hours of operation - Open daily
Phone - 707-963-0717
Address - 2950 Sage Canyon Road, St. Helena, California 94574
Web Site - www.nicheliniwinery.com
Appointment required - Monday - Friday only
Tasting fee - Complimentary

Nichelini Winery has been producing outstanding wines for years. As with the other wineries on this tour, this rustic gem is located in a beautiful rural scenic area. Check the winery web site for directions.

<u>Rustridge Winery</u> - *Wine Tasting* - 2:30 p.m. to 3:15 p.m.

Rustridge was mentioned in *Option No. 1* above. Check it out for details.

If time left over after Rustridge, feel free to explore the Chiles Valley area around Lake Hennessey...or visit another winery in the lower valley region.

Final thoughts on "Sample Day Tours"

As previously noted, the ten *Sample Day Tours* highlighted can be easily taken by anyone. However, the wineries listed only scratch the surface. With so many in the area, one could easily spend weeks exploring them all. Whether spending a day or two, or visiting longer, by now you should be aware of one thing. *Prior planning is a must.* In addition, if you've got this far, you now possess the knowledge to plan your own day in the Napa Valley. For example, let's say you've got several wineries in mind that didn't appear in any of the *Ten Sample Day Tours.* No problem. *Build your own tour … Get a good tour map prior to your visit, go on line and do some research, make any required appointments well in advance, and apply the time saving tips you've learned here.* By doing so, you can plan your own unique *Napa Valley Experience.*

One last point about *"building your own tour."* As indicated throughout the book, it's always prudent to obtain a *Current Winery Map* prior to your visit. But remember, there are over 300 wineries in the region. Most maps don't list them all for several reasons. Many choose not to be on maps. They may be open to the public on an appointment only basis, or even a walk-in basis, but just choose not to be listed. Still others are small family owned wineries not open to the public. So remember, if a winery isn't listed, it doesn't necessarily mean you can't visit. If you have a winery in mind, find their phone number or punch in their name on line to see if they have a web site.

Do whatever it takes to get in touch with them. You may be surprised to find they would love to have you drop by to sample their wines.

Part 13

Winery Addendum

"Off the Beaten Path" Wineries

Amizetta, Burgess, Casa Nuestra, Chappellet, Chateau Potelle, Graeser, Hans Faden, Kuleto Estate, Nichelini, Pride Mountain, Rustridge, Smith - Madrone. Check your tour map for locations.

Lower Napa Valley "Carneros Region" Wineries

The *Carneros Region* is known for producing outstanding Pinot Noir and Chardonnay wines, plus Sparkling Wines. Facilities in this region include *Acacia, Artesa, Domaine Carneros, Madonna Estate, and Saintsbury*. Again, refer to your map for locations.

More Wineries to consider

The following is a partial list of additional wineries to consider. Some have already been mentioned. The list is by no means an endorsement of any facility. In addition, it would be inappropriate to list over 300 wineries since many are not open to the public. I've personally taken hundreds of people on wine tours to many on the list. I suggest going to the Napa web site to check them out. Once there, click on the *wineries* category, then look around until you find the facility your looking for. In addition, please consider these points regarding the list. Periodically, a winery may merge with another and change its name. On occasion, a winery goes out of business. A winery may also be sold, the new owner desiring a name change. At the time of publication, the following facilities were doing business under the names listed:

Acacia, Alpha Omega, Amizetta, Andretti, Artesa, Arger Martucci, August Briggs, Baldacci, Bell, Benessere, Bennett Lane, Beringer, Beaulieu, Black Stallion, Burgess, "CIA" - Culinary Institute of America, Calistoga Cellars, Cakebread, Caymus, Charles Krug, Chateau Montelena, Chimney Rock, Cliff Lede, Clos Pegase, Conn Creek, Conn Valley, COPIA, Cosentino, Clos Du Val, Cuvaison, Darioush, Del Dotto Caves, Diamond Oaks, Domaine Carneros, Domaine Chandon, Duckhorn, Ehlers Estate, Esquisse, Flora Springs, Folie a Deux, Franciscan, Frank Family, Freemark Abbey, Frogs Leap, Goosecross, Graeser, Grgich Hills, Groth, Hall, Hans Fahden, Heitz, Hess, Honig, Jarvis, Joseph Phelps, Judd's Hill, Kirkland Ranch, Kuleto Estate, Laird, Louis Martini, Markham, Merryvale, Milat, Miner Family, Monticello, Mumm, Napa Cellars, Nichelini, Nicholson Ranch, Opus 1, Paraduxx, Peju, Pina, Pine Ridge, Plumpjack, Prager, Pride Mountain, Provenance, Raymond, Regusci, Robert Craig, Robert Mondavi, Robert Sinskey, Rombauer, Rubicon Estate, Rutherford Grove, Rutherford Hill, Rutherford Ranch, Rustridge, St. Clement, St. Supery, Schramsberg, Sequoia Grove, Shafer, Signorello, Silver Oak, Silverado, Silver Rose, Smith-Madrone, Spring Mountain Vineyard, Staglin Family, Stags Leap Wine Cellars, Stelzner, Sterling, Summers, Sutter Home, Swanson, Trefethen, Trinchero Family Estates, Twomey, V. Sattui, Van Der Heyden, Vine Cliff, Whitehall Lane, William Hill, ZD, Zahtila

Final Word from the Author

Many informative travel guides have been written about *California's Napa Valley Wine Country*. However, few if any have targeted the specific needs of the *short term visitor*. Yet traditionally, most visitors to the area usually spend only one or two days in the region. During many years conducting wine tours, I was able to gain the knowledge necessary to help such visitors eliminate most problems experienced prior to and during brief visits. Hopefully, the enclosed information has been helpful in planning your trip. In addition, with so many other things to do in the area besides visiting wineries, I would encourage you to stay much longer. Wishing you a safe and rewarding *Napa Valley Experience!*

J. Michael Orr

Directory

(listed in random order)

J. Michael Orr c/o Napa Valley Art Studio
Winery Tour Maps, Wine Country Art Posters, Tour Itineraries
Additional copies *"A Day or Two in the Napa Valley"*
1-800-923-7635 - 1-775-345-7682
Fax- 1-775-345-9817
www.napavalleytourmap.com
E mail - napavalleytour@sbcglobal.net

General Information - All Categories *www.napavalley.com*

Napa Valley Conference & Visitors Bureau
707-226-7459 or 707-226-5813
www.napavalley.org

Napa Chamber of Commerce - 707-226-7455
www.napachamber.com

Napa Sonoma Wine Country Visitors Center - 707-642-0686

St. Helena Chamber of Commerce - 707-963-4456
www.sthelenachamber.com

Yountville Chamber of Commerce - 707-944-0904
www.yountville.com

Calistoga Chamber of Commerce - 707-942-6333
www.calistogachamber.com

COPIA - 707-259-1600 *www.copia.org*

Napa Valley Museum - 707-944-0500
www.napavalleymuseum.com

Napa Valley Mustard Festival - 707-259-9020

April in Carneros - 1-800-654-WINE

Old Faithful Geyser - 707-942-6463
www.oldfaithfulgeyser.com

Marine World Theme Park - 707-643-6722
www.marineworldvallejo.com

PB&J's - 707-226-5867   *www.partyatpbjs.com*

Petrified Forest - Calistoga - 707-942-6667
www.petrifiedforest.org

Jelly Belly Candy Company - 800-953-5592
www.jellybelly.com

Napa Valley Wine Train - 707-253-2111
www.winetrain.com

Bay Link Ferry - 707-643-3779   *www.baylinkferry.com*

Vintage 1870 Shopping Complex - 707-944-2451
www.vintage1870.com

Data sources for Wine Magazines, "Wine Ratings" and other valuable information:
www.wineenthusiast.com
www.winebusiness.com

Silverado Trail Wineries Association - 866-844-9463
Lists over 35 wineries along the rural Silverado Trail
www.silveradotrail.com

Index

Wineries Visited / Wines Tasted

Contact Persons / Phone Numbers

Other Notes